I have known Greg Koukl for a quarter of a century as a smart, well-educated man of integrity with a tender heart for God. I've enjoyed his previous writings, but *The Story of Reality* is clearly his best and most important book to date. I couldn't put it down. Koukl carries on a conversation with the reader, presenting the big elements of the Christian Story, providing reasons for believing the Story, and contrasting it, when appropriate, with alternative narratives. The book has a wonderful feel of authenticity. I highly recommend it for believers who want to be encouraged and instructed, and it's an excellent give-away for an open unbeliever.

J. P. MORELAND, Distinguished Professor of Philosophy,
Talbot School of Theology, Biola University

Greg Koukl is a master communicator! *The Story of Reality* is a beautifully crafted description of the Christian worldview, written in an accessible, winsome, and well-reasoned manner. If you're curious about why Christians see the world the way we do, or you're a believer who simply wants to communicate Christianity in an articulate way to others, this book is for you!

LEE STROBEL, bestselling author of *The Case for Christ*
and *The Case for Grace*

We're not likely to glean the point of our existence from CNN. It takes the greatest story ever told—and a great storyteller—to steal us away from our dead-end plots and to display the richness of reality as Greg Koukl does here. These are the big questions, and *The Story of Reality* answers them in a sharp, winsome, and accessible way. Read it, and then give it to a friend!

MICHAEL HORTON, J. Gresham Machen Professor of Theology,
Westminster Seminary California; author of *Pilgrim Theology*

The Story of Reality is the clearest explanation the Christian worldview I've ever read, written in a style everyone can understand. More than any other time in history, it's essential that followers of Christ clearly understand what we believe, why we believe it, how it benefits our lives, and the best ways to share it with others. Fortunately, my friend Greg Koukl has given us this book at just the right moment. He has brilliantly given us a simple tool we all can use in a culture that has lost touch with reality.

RICK WARREN, author of *The Purpose Driven Life*

The Story of Reality is a delightful and bold book. Greg Koukl has masterfully captured the heart of the Christian story in a way that is clarifying and insightful for believers but also eye-opening and thought-provoking for nonbelievers. *The Story of Reality* is a book worth reading carefully, discussing with friends, and ultimately passing on to others.

SEAN MCDOWELL, Ph.D. professor at Biola University;
author of more than fifteen books, including *A New Kind of Apologist*

When I looked into Koukl's *Story of Reality*, I thought, "This is not how I would say this." I would have used more technical terms, added quite a bit of history, expanded it by a couple of hundred pages, and put in about a thousand footnotes. So readers can rejoice that, instead, Greg Koukl is the right man to tell the story in such a clear, concise, and conversational way. This book explains the central ideas of Christianity and answers questions people are really asking.

FRED SANDERS, Torrey Honors Institute, Biola University;
author of *The Deep Things of God*

When I first read *The Story of Reality*, I knew I was reading a modern classic. Like C. S. Lewis before him, Greg Koukl has written a masterful, measured, intelligent, and insightful book—a must-read for anyone who wants to understand Christianity and it's unique ability to explain the way the world really is. Greg will enlighten and inspire you, just as he's inspired me as my mentor for many years. *The Story of Reality* is a book you'll read more than once. It will take its rightful place alongside other Christian classics on your bookshelf.

J. WARNER WALLACE, author of *Cold-Case Christianity*,
God's Crime Scene, and *Forensic Faith*

Not since *Mere Christianity* has a book so wonderfully told the Story of Reality. The Greatest Story Ever Told is true, and Greg Koukl tells it in such a compelling way that I'm recommending you not only experience it but give a copy to everyone you care about. Why? Because *The Story of Reality* is not just the Christian Story—it is your Story whether you believe it or not.

FRANK TUREK, author of *I Don't Have Enough Faith to Be an Atheist*

The Story of Reality is perfect as an introduction to Christianity for new Christians, for older Christians who've never grasped the "big picture," and even for non-Christians wondering if the Christian worldview really makes sense. Greg Koukl masterfully explains and defends what Christianity is—an accurate description of reality from the beginning of time through its end, and not just one of many valid worldviews—and he does so with the simplicity and clarity that is the hallmark of Koukl's writings. This book is a fresh alternative to the distorted picture of Christianity fostered by the politically correct crowd that is naively accepted by so many.

MICHAEL LICONA, Associate Professor of Theology,
Houston Baptist University; author of *The Resurrection of Jesus*

Nothing is more important than knowing reality. There are many stories, but only one essential Story of reality itself. That is what we must know. In straightforward and interesting language, Mr. Koukl tells that story truthfully and skillfully. He deserves a close reading by anyone who is uncertain about who they are and where they are going.

DOUGLAS GROOTHUIS, Ph.D., Professor of Philosophy,
Denver Seminary; author of *Christian Apologetics:
A Comprehensive Case for Biblical Faith*

This primer on a Christian outlook on life by Greg Koukl covers an incredibly large number of the pithiest issues in an amazingly small number of pages. Time and again I wondered, "Now how is Greg going to work his way through this question quickly and nontechnically?" But the thoughtful, succinct, and quick-moving answer that followed never disappointed and was handled amazingly. It is not an exaggeration to call this treatment C. S. Lewis–like in a number of ways. Those who pay attention to the fast pace will later be astonished at how far they have come. I recommend it highly.

GARY R. HABERMAS, Distinguished Research Professor and Chair,
Dept. of Philosophy, Liberty University; author of *The Case for the
Resurrection of Jesus*

My friend Greg Koukl is known as a man whose ambition is to be pleasing to God—and his newest work, *The Story of Reality*, certainly is ambitious. How can one cover "the reason for everything" in a single manuscript? Well, Greg tackles the challenge valiantly and courageously, addressing the heartfelt plea of every person who asks, "Why am I here? What is so important about life?" Thoughtful, provocative, and intellectually stimulating, Greg walks the reader through the big issues of life, giving answers that are truly worthy of consideration by the toughest skeptic. I highly recommend this stirring book by a most remarkable apologist!

JONI EARECKSON TADA, Joni and Friends International Disability Center

Greg Koukl thinks you deserve answers to your "why" questions about reality, and he offers them with wit and compassion. *The Story of Reality* brings the greatest story ever told to life in all its brilliant simplicity.

JEFF MYERS, Ph.D., President, Summit Ministries

In a day when so many people find the Bible's message to be anything but sensible, Greg Koukl's *The Story of Reality* does a superb job of showing how much sense it really makes after all—first, by putting the story in order, beginning with God and moving from there through man's creation, man's problem, and God's solution; and second, by showing through solid reasoning that the biblical story is more believable—and thus more sensible—than any other way of looking at reality. For anyone who wants to be able either to understand the story better or to explain it more clearly, this book is essential.

TOM GILSON, author of *True Reason: Confronting the Irrationality of the New Atheism*

Writing a small book on all that ever was, is, or will be is, needless to say, a daunting task. But if anybody could pull it off, it is Greg Koukl. And his *Story of Reality* does it better than any small book I can remember reading. This book is not intended for great philosophers or theologians—although any of them would benefit greatly by reading it. This book is for everyone who simply has the slightest desire to know with a great deal of certainty who we are, why we're here, what this is all about, and where we're going. If a person wants a succinct, straightforward, and deeply knowledgeable answer to those questions (and I'm pretty sure that's everybody), this is the book I would have to recommend. This work is a fantastic gift to the Church! I hope church leaders understand how important it is—and how life changing it can be for so many in their congregations.

CRAIG J. HAZEN, Ph.D., Founder and Director, Graduate Program in Christian Apologetics, Biola University; author of *Five Sacred Crossings*

Greg Koukl is one of the clearest and most accessible Christian communicators I know. Telling the big Story of God's purpose and actions in history, Greg masterfully demonstrates why no other story but Christianity can account for the way the world is and why it matters. Common sense, a logical approach, and years of experience in putting the puzzle pieces together in his own life, make Greg an ideal guide for others seeking to piece together the true Story of reality for themselves.

JUSTIN BRIERLEY, host of the *Unbelievable?* radio show
and podcast

If you're looking for something fresh in the conversation about faith and culture, *The Story of Reality* is for you. Offering more than just a series of propositions and claims, Koukl weaves propositional truth into a story that we can all relate to and find ourselves in. Easy to read yet intellectually stimulating, this book is worth your time.

ABDU MURRAY, North American Director of Ravi Zacharias
International Ministries; author of *Grand Central Question:
Answering the Critical Concerns of the Major Worldviews*

Greg has done us all a great service by giving a fresh answer to our oldest questions. In simple yet insightful and profound ways, *The Story of Reality* will help you understand all the "whys" that matter most to us. Whether you want to begin your own personal journey toward understanding or be sharpened in your ability to help others as they wrestle with timeless curiosities, your time in this book will serve you well.

TODD WAGNER, Pastor, Watermark Church, Dallas

Also by Gregory Koukl

Tactics: A Game Plan for Discussing Your Christian Convictions

Tactics Study Guide with DVD

Relativism: Feet Firmly Planted in Mid-Air

THE STORY OF
REALITY

HOW THE WORLD BEGAN, HOW IT ENDS, AND EVERYTHING IMPORTANT THAT HAPPENS IN BETWEEN

GREGORY KOUKL

FOREWORD BY NANCY PEARCEY

ZONDERVAN

The Story of Reality
Copyright © 2017 by Gregory Koukl

This title is also available as a Zondervan ebook.

This title is also available as a Zondervan audio edition.

Requests for information should be addressed to:
Zondervan, 3900 *Sparks Dr. SE, Grand Rapids, Michigan* 49546

ISBN 978-0-310-52504-2

Published in association with the literary agency of Mark Sweeney & Associates,
Bonita Springs, Florida 34135.

Art direction: Tammy Johnson
Interior design: Kait Lamphere
Editorial: Ryan Pazdur, Taylor Kemmeter, Bob Hudson

Printed in the United States of America

17 18 19 20 21 22 23 24 25 26 27 /DCI/ 15 14 13 12 11 10 9 8 7 6 5 4 3 2

To Eva, my little Morning Star
That you might daily walk closely in friendship
with the gracious God of reality

Contents

Part Three: Jesus

Part Four: Cross

Part Five: Resurrection

Foreword

ONE OF FRANCIS SCHAEFFER'S most memorable sayings was that Christianity does not start with "Jesus saves you from your sins." It starts with "In the beginning, God created the heavens and the earth."

Schaeffer's point was that Christianity cannot be reduced to a tract or a technique for getting "saved." It is a comprehensive account of the structure of reality, a rational and real-world account of the history of the universe, a verifiable storyline of the unfolding of the cosmos.

In this book, you will read Greg Koukl's recounting of that storyline. In a simple and engaging manner, he lays out the context and background information that allows us to make sense of the message of salvation.

It is perfectly true that Jesus came to save us from that deforming disorder called "sin." But starting with that theme is like going into a movie theater halfway through the film. You don't know who the characters are, you can't figure out the plot, and you are constantly guessing at the events leading up to that point. Most important, you cannot appreciate the depth and complexity of the problem that needs to be solved.

That illustrates a major reason the message of Christianity no longer makes sense to many people today. They are no longer familiar with the first part of the drama. As a result, not surprisingly, they cannot make sense of key concepts such as sin and salvation.

The New Testament apostles faced the same challenge. On one hand, when talking to Jewish people, the apostles could count on a certain background knowledge of Scripture and the history of Israel. Their audiences knew who God was, understood concepts like sin and atonement, and were looking forward to the coming of the Messiah. The apostles could simply lay out their arguments why Jesus fit the criteria for the expected Messiah.

By contrast, when addressing an audience of gentiles, who had no background knowledge of the Hebrew Scripture, the apostles had to begin at a much more foundational level. In Acts, we see Paul speaking to gentiles living in an area that is now part of Turkey. He starts by laying a groundwork of God as the Creator, "the living God, who made the heavens and the earth and the sea and everything in them." How has God revealed himself to these people without Scripture? Through the created order: He "did not leave himself without witness, for he did good by giving you rains from heaven and fruitful seasons, satisfying your hearts with food and gladness" (Acts 14:15, 17). Knowledge of God is accessible through creation.

The most famous example is Paul addressing an audience of Greek philosophers—Stoics and Epicureans—in the city of Athens. Again he builds his argument on what everyone can know about God through the created order. In Acts 17, he begins by proclaiming that the deity he is talking about is "the God who made the world and everything in it," who "is the Lord of heaven and earth."

Paul makes it clear that he is not talking about just another idol, like the many idols scattered throughout Athens. No, this God is a transcendent Creator—self-existent, self-sufficient, autonomous, independent—who "does not live in temples made by human hands. And he is not served by human hands, as if he needed anything."

From there, Paul proceeds to build the Christian worldview one logical step at a time. This Creator is the one who "gives everyone life and breath and everything else." It was he who created the human race: "From one man he made all the nations, that they should inhabit the whole earth." And like a parent who gives birth to children, he aspires to enjoy a relationship with the people he created: "God did this so that they would seek him and perhaps reach out for him and find him, though he is not far from any one of us." When addressing Greeks, instead of quoting the Hebrew Scripture, Paul quotes well-known Greek poets: "'For in him we live and move and have our being.' As some of your own poets have said, 'We are his offspring.'"

Logically, if humans are God's "offspring," the implication is that God must be a personal being, as we are. The underlying principle is that the cause must be equal to the effect. The source of human life must have at least the same capacities that humans have. Therefore the Creator cannot be a thing or substance: "We should not think that the divine being is like gold or silver or stone," an allusion to the idols familiar to the Athenians. In fact, the origin of human life cannot be anything that humans have created—it cannot be "an image made by human design and skill."

After making sure his Greek audience understands who God is, only then does Paul take them to the moral implications. If a personal God created us as personal beings, then it is logical to conclude that we stand in a personal relationship with him. In fact, we have a moral obligation to him, owing him respect and fidelity, just as human offspring have an obligation to honor the parents who brought them into the world.

Moreover, because honoring God is a moral obligation, failure to fulfill that obligation constitutes a moral fault, an ethical breach. We are guilty of breaking a cosmic law, and the proper response is to heal the breach—what the Bible calls repentance: "Now he commands all people everywhere to repent." And God has sent Jesus as both Savior and Judge, giving evidence of his identity by raising him from the dead: "He has set a day when he will judge the world with justice by the man he has appointed. He has given proof of this to everyone by raising him from the dead."

Notice that it is only after laying the groundwork of who God is, who we are, and our relationship to him that Paul explains sin and guilt, then Jesus and the resurrection.

Evangelicals often put things backward, seeking to persuade people of their sin when they have no idea yet what the term means. Small wonder that the typical response to their message is, "Don't call me a sinner! Why do I owe this God anything? Besides, I'm not even sure God exists."

As you read this book by Greg Koukl, you will find your perspective gently being reoriented. He helps you to put first things first, enabling you to perceive how reasonably and cogently everything fits together and falls into place. The Christian worldview is logically coherent. Each principle follows the one that went before, like an expertly composed symphony or a carefully crafted storyline.

Do not be fooled by the simplicity of Koukl's presentation. He is a careful craftsmen whose clear, lucid prose sounds almost as if he is telling a once-upon-a-time story. But his point is just the opposite: The Bible is not a fairy tale crafted by ancient people to give a sense of meaning to life. It is an account of reality. He calls it a story only because, amazingly, it turns out that reality itself is structured like a great drama: It has a beginning and an end; it features a struggle between good and evil; it reaches a climax and then resolves into a denouement and a finale.

The cosmos is not just a succession of brute facts. It is the plotline of a grand story that God is telling through the verifiable events of history.

Because of Koukl's transparent prose, you may be tempted to read this book quickly. Resist that temptation. In reality he is communicating the same complex ideas that theologians and philosophers present through polysyllabic terms and labyrinthine paragraphs. You will learn about some of the most intractable debates that have filled scholarly textbooks for centuries—but you will do so with the ease and pleasure of reading a novel. Koukl makes the plotline of biblical history come alive. This is a book that begs to be read slowly and savored.

I will end with another saying from Francis Schaeffer. He observed that the gospel is complex enough to keep theologians and philosophers busy writing learned tomes for years, and yet simple enough for a child to grasp the essentials. Greg Koukl has mastered the art of writing in a simple, straightforward style that can be grasped by anyone, while nevertheless communicating profound truths.

I do not want to keep you any longer from a reading experience that will delight and transform. Enter into *The Story of Reality*.

Nancy Pearcey
Houston, October 2016

Preface

THE FIRST QUESTION any of us learns to ask about anything—and we usually learn to ask it quite early in life—is "Why?"

Children ask it incessantly about all sorts of things. We usually don't mind because we know their questions generally have answers, and in many cases (with the easier questions) we know what the answers are. Put simply, there are reasons for the way things are, and it's the most natural thing in the world for us to try to figure out what those reasons might be. It's one of the first things we learn.

I want you to fix that point in your mind from the outset: *There are reasons for the way things are.* If there were no reasons, it would make no sense to ask "Why?" But the question almost always seems like a proper one.

As we get older, asking "Why?" goes deeper into the heart of things. We begin asking the question not of any individual thing, but of the whole thing. What is the reason for *everything*? Why am I here? Why is anything here? Why is anything important or good or beautiful? Why?

The farther along we get, the more frequently we ask the question, until we either find an answer that satisfies us or we get weary asking and decide there is no answer at all, so we might as well stop wondering. When that happens, it is usually a very dark day because it certainly *seems* like the question is a proper one and it *seems* like it is the most important one and it *seems* like there is more to life than aimless activity. So to settle for anything less is a desolate moment for the soul.

There are answers to life's most basic questions, though, and in this book I want to give them to you.

I know the answers not because I'm especially clever and figured them out on my own. Of course, some things you can safely conclude if you think carefully about the clues (more on that later). But the best way to get accurate insight into any story is to let the author tell you himself. Yes, life is a kind of story and this Story has an Author. This is one thing that's fairly easy to figure out from the clues.

In this book I want to tell you that story—the Story of reality—and help you see your place in it.

Gregory Koukl

REALITY

CHAPTER 1

Confusion

I WANT TO TELL YOU the story about how the world began, how the world ends, and everything deeply important that happens in between. It's a tale many already know but few understand, even those who call the Story their own. This story is not a fairy tale, but rather it is the Story all fairy tales are really about.[1] Indeed, almost every tale ever written is an echo of this story embedded deep within our hearts. Yet this story is not a tale at all, since the Story is true.

This is the Story of reality—a story about things that really happened or, in some parts, things that are going to happen. It started a long time ago and will end (probably) long after you and I are gone. It is a story so wonderful in some places—some might even say magical—and so frightening in other places, it is hard to imagine it can be true. But when we think about it carefully, we realize deep inside that it all makes perfect sense.

There is a problem, though, with attempting to tell the Story. The effort will probably be misunderstood.

Once I was sitting on an airplane next to a stockbroker. He asked me what I did for a living, and I told him I was a writer. When he asked what I wrote about, immediately I faced a difficulty. I wanted to tell him that I write and talk about religion, specifically Christian religion, but I didn't want him to make a mistake many people make when they think about those two things.

Most people nowadays would not say the religious stories believers believe are actually false. (It would be impolite to put it that way and might even be considered intolerant). At the same time, though, they do not think they're really true, either, in any deep sense of the word.

Instead, people are tempted to think of religion as a kind of spiritual fantasy club—true for you, but not necessarily true for me. Find the club you like—the one that meets your personal needs, that gives you rules to live by that are respectable but not too demanding, that warms your heart with a feeling of spirituality. That's the point of religion. Do not, however, confuse religious stories with reality. They don't give you the kind of information about the world that, say, science does. Yes, believing in God is useful to a point, but religion taken too seriously is, in some ways, like believing in Santa Claus—quaint if you're a child but unbecoming of an adult.

I am convinced this is a completely misguided approach to religion, and I did not want the stockbroker (or anyone else, for that matter) thinking this is what I had in mind—that my faith is an exercise in spiritual wishful thinking, the kind of delusion Karl Marx once called the "opiate of the people." My comments to the stockbroker, then, were informed by a particular way of understanding Christianity, a way even many Christians have not fully grasped.

Here I need to ask you a rhetorical question. It's a question I don't want you to answer (I'll answer it for you), but one I want you to think about as if you did have to answer it. Here is that question: What *is* Christianity?

Some say Christianity is a religious system people follow. Others say it is a guide to living a fulfilling life or maybe a way of finding peace with God or maybe a system of ethical principles to live by. Some might say Christianity is not really a religion at all but rather a relationship with God or a relationship with Jesus. This way of putting it might be confusing to some, but I think I understand what those who say this are getting at.

These answers all have some truth to them as far as they go, I guess. The problem is, I do not think they go far enough. They are all too thin, in a certain sense. Each is a look at Christianity from the inside, so to speak, from the perspective of the Christian living out his or her individual beliefs or personal faith. That is certainly part of it, and I think these answers would have made complete sense to the stockbroker. But there is something missing.

The answer to the question "What is Christianity?" turns out to be much bigger than any one of those things because it includes something important from the outside as well as the inside. The way Jesus understood religion was not simply as a private, spiritual view or as a subjective source of ethics or even as a personalized relationship with God. Jesus understood religion first from the outside, not from the inside.

Here is what I am getting at. The correct answer to the question "What is Christianity?" is this: *Christianity is a picture of reality.*[2] It is an account or a description or a depiction of the way things actually are. It is not just a view from the inside (a Christian's personal feelings or religious beliefs or spiritual affections or ethical views or "relationship" with God). It is also a view of the outside. It is a view of the world out there, of how the world really is in itself.

Put another way, Christianity is a worldview. The Christian view is not the only way of viewing the world, of course. It has competition. Every religion and every secular philosophy claims to represent reality in a true and accurate way. Indeed, every person has a view like this of some sort. Everyone has in his or her mind a story about the way the world actually is, even if they haven't thought about it much or worked out all the details.

This story-in-their-mind is what people are referring to when they say they have certain beliefs about things like meaning, value, purpose, and significance. Or they will say, "This is the way I look at things" or "This is what I think the correct view is" or "There ought to be a law about that" or "I don't think the government is taking this in the right direction" or "That was the right thing to do in that situation." Every statement like these is informed by an understanding of the way people believe the world actually is. It is their belief system. If they did not have a basic story in their minds, they would have a difficult time making any of the important decisions people are faced with in life.

In this sense, there is no difference between an atheist and a religious person. None. Each believes particular things to be true about the world. I am not using the word *believe* here like some people use the word *faith*, that is, a *mere* belief with no thought, rationale, or justification behind it. I do think that happens with religious people, and I also think that happens with atheists, but that is not what I'm talking about here.

A person's belief, in my sense of the word, is simply his view of some detail of the world that he holds to be accurate. That's all. And both scientists and saints alike have beliefs of this sort. There's nothing unusual going on here.

Now of course, just because someone believes things about the world does not mean they *know* their beliefs are true. That is something else entirely. But they still *think* their beliefs are true, otherwise they would not believe them. They would believe different things and think those things true instead.

Since everyone—religious person, atheist, scientist, skeptic—believes his beliefs are true, it has always struck me as odd when some have been faulted simply for thinking their views correct. They've even been labeled intolerant or bigoted for doing so. But what is the alternative? The person objecting thinks his own views correct as well, which is why he's objecting. Both parties in the conversation think they're right and the other wrong. Why, then, is only the religious person (usually) branded a bigot for doing so?

So, all of us have beliefs about the world we think are accurate. All of us have a worldview picture—at least a rudimentary one—forming in our minds, even if we are not consciously aware of it. Every religion tells a story of reality. Every philosophy and every individual outlook on life is a take on the way someone thinks the world actually is. There is no escaping it. These stories are meant to bring order to our beliefs, to explain the "pieces" of reality we encounter in life, whether big things or little things, important or inconsequential.

All worldviews are not equal, though. Some have pieces that seem to fit together (internally) better than others, and some have pieces that seem to fit reality (externally) better than others. If they are good stories—that is, if they explain many things, especially the most important things, in a way consistent with our normal encounters with the world—then we have more confidence the stories are accurate, which is just another way of saying the worldview is true, at least those parts that fit well.

CHAPTER 2

Puzzle

EVERY WORLDVIEW HAS FOUR ELEMENTS. They help us understand how the parts of a person's worldview story fit together. These four parts are called creation, fall, redemption, and restoration.

Creation tells us how things began, where everything came from (including us), the reason for our origins, and what ultimate reality is like. *Fall* describes the problem (since we all know something has gone wrong with the world). *Redemption* gives us the solution, the way to fix what went wrong. *Restoration* describes what the world would look like once the repair takes place.

Put in personal terms, worldviews help us answer the basic questions each of us struggles with sooner or later in our lives if we pause to think about the really important things: Where did we come from? What is our problem? What is the solution? How will things end for us?

You might have noticed that these four words describing the elements of a worldview have a religious ring to them. There's a reason for that. Though more secular words might be substituted (I'll do that in a bit), I think it's important for you to see that since worldviews represent such a fundamental understanding of all of the important things about the world, a person's worldview is really a part of his religion, even if it doesn't include gods, temples, bibles, rituals, or the like. In this sense, even atheists have a religion, though they probably would not use that word to describe it.

Every worldview means to tell a story like this one, a story of reality.

It means to make sense of the way the world actually is—the world as we find it—not simply the world as we wish it to be.

I want you to see something else about this worldview picture. When you were younger you probably worked on puzzles. Maybe you still do. Puzzles are a good way to think about worldviews since they are made up of lots of individual pieces too. When the pieces are fit together properly, you're able to see the big picture clearly.

Of course, to get the picture precisely right you have to work with all the right pieces. For example, God and Jesus and Moses and the Law and grace and the cross and faith (and a whole bunch of other things) are all important pieces of the Christian puzzle. You can immediately see, I hope, that if you are missing pieces (if there are important parts you don't know about) or if you have pieces of other worldview puzzles mixed in by accident, you will not get an accurate sense of things. That can be a problem.

But here's the bigger difficulty. Dump a puzzle box at your feet and you'll see what the Christian puzzle looks like for most believers. It's a pile of pieces. They've never put the pieces of their puzzle together in an orderly way allowing them to see the big picture. As a result, they do not know if they are missing important pieces. They also do not know if there are pieces of other puzzles—bits of other worldviews—mixed in by accident that don't fit into their picture. Or they might get confused when other worldviews take some of the Christian pieces and try to fit them into their own worldview pictures.

Pieces from one puzzle usually cannot be mixed with pieces of another because they are made for different pictures. You can't take, for example, the unique value of human beings (a central piece of the biblical worldview and the foundation for human rights) and force fit it into the Hindu worldview. It will not work. There is no place for it to fit. They are different puzzles with different pieces.

In the same way, reincarnation makes sense in Hinduism but not in Christianity. Again, there is no place in the biblical view for that puzzle piece to fit. It's like trying to put a carburetor on a computer.

Both problems (missing pieces and wrong pieces) make it difficult for Christians (or anyone else, for that matter) to put the puzzle of Christianity together correctly. Even with all the right pieces, few Christians have ever assembled their puzzle in an accurate way to make sense of the whole thing. As a result, lots of well-meaning, but untutored (and, therefore, gullible) Christians do not see reality clearly and have gotten into trouble.

So how do we figure out the way the pieces fit together properly? If you are a puzzle person, you know there's a trick. Though some consider it cheating, it's okay here. You look at the cover. Seeing the whole thing at once helps you know where the individual parts fit in. If you do not know what the big picture looks like beforehand, it will be much harder to assemble it from the parts.

So far, I have been saying Christianity is first and foremost a picture of reality, a view of the way the world is—a worldview. I've suggested a way of understanding what a worldview is like. It's like a picture puzzle you piece together. You need to have all the right pieces with no foreign pieces mixed in, and you need to put those pieces together properly to see the big picture clearly. I have also been using another way of understanding worldview. A worldview is like a story, and nowadays I think this is the best way to put it.

When you think about it, every story, if it is a good one, has four parts. It has a beginning that sets the stage, telling you who the main characters are and how the story gets rolling. Then something goes wrong. There is conflict that makes the story interesting. The main part of most stories tells how that conflict gets corrected, how the wrong gets fixed. That solution brings a final resolution—writers call it the *denouement*—where the parts of the plot resolve themselves in a satisfying ending ("They lived happily ever after"). Maybe you've noticed that the basic parts of a good story actually match the basic parts of a worldview: beginning (creation), conflict (fall), conflict resolution (redemption), and ending (restoration).

The Christian Story is like many other great stories in that it deals with the great issues all people struggle with and the great questions everyone asks. It's a story about peace shattered by rebellion, about love and betrayal, about self-sacrifice, and about redemption. All of our deepest aspirations, all of our longings, all of our hopes and even our struggles—all of the conflicts in all of history are all tied to this story.

Put another way, Christianity is the Story of how the world began, why the world is the way it is, what role we play in the drama, and how all the plotlines of the Story are resolved in the end.

CHAPTER 3

True Story

NOW I WANT TO REVIEW a point I have already been making that is so important for you to understand, I want to explain it again from a different direction so you do not miss it.

The Christian Story starts out a long, long time ago, long before Jesus. How long ago is a matter of debate, but that does not concern us here. One thing that does concern us is this: The Christian Story is different from other stories in a significant way. This story does not start with the words, "Once upon a time." Why? Because this story is not meant to be understood as a fairy tale or a myth.

When my eldest daughter was young, she read *The Chronicles of Narnia*. After finishing the first book she asked me, "Papa, is the story about the wardrobe and Peter and Susan and Lucy and Edmund and the lion a true story?"

"No, it's not," I told her. "Some stories are true, and some stories are not true. The story about Narnia is fiction." (I did tell her, though, that some fictional stories like Narnia are actually *about* true stories, even though the stories themselves are not true.) The Christian Story, I was careful to point out, is not like the Narnia story. It isn't make-believe. It is a true story.

Now, when I say this story is a true story, I'm using the word *true* in its ordinary sense. I don't mean "true *for me*." I mean "true *to reality*." I mean the things the Story describes actually exist and the events in the Story really happened (or, in some places, are yet to happen).

This is the same as saying, as I did earlier, that Christianity is a picture of reality. This is the Story of the way the world really is. That's the kind of story I'm telling. It's history, not fiction. This was the point I was trying to make with the stockbroker. I didn't want him to think the Story was my personal spiritual fantasy, my religious fairy tale, or my make-believe-to-make-me-feel-happy kind of story.

This point is important for another reason. One of our deepest questions about our world is "What went wrong?" We know the world is broken, but we wonder how that happened, and we want to fix it. Those two issues are related. Answer the first and you might be able to answer the second.

That's why a myth or a fairy tale simply will not do for the Christian Story. Make-believe accounts do not actually explain anything. They only illustrate problems in clever, imaginative ways. When a boy asks his father how he got the scar on his face, if his father begins with the words "once upon a time," the boy immediately knows his father is not giving him an answer to his question. Only a true-life experience can leave a true-life scar.

The world is wounded, this we know. Answering the question of how it got to be wounded requires more than a myth. It requires an accurate account of reality. This point about reality applies to every detail of the story I am telling. The narrative is history, and if it is not, it explains nothing.

So, I mean to be telling you the true Story of reality. Nowadays, however, there are many people who think this entire discussion is irrelevant because they think such a story cannot be told. They have heard that no story like this—no big story, no all-encompassing story—can ever be true (or at least *known* to be true, which amounts to the same thing). And some are tempted to believe it.

The reason, they say, is because it's hard to be confident we can know anything at all about the world "out there"—that is, about the way the world is *in itself* as opposed to our own personal *beliefs* about it. For them, everything is belief and nothing is knowledge. This is a view you'll encounter, ironically, at universities—places of higher education where you learn there is nothing you can actually know.

Does this view strike you as unusual? It strikes me that way. In fact, it strikes me as obviously false. Here's why. Put simply, there are lots of things we know, and we know that we know them. Reality has a way of getting our attention and teaching us about itself. This is amazingly simple to demonstrate.

A few years ago I was with my family in Washington, D.C., a wildly complex city laid out like a square wheel with broken spokes making an angular maze that is a nightmare to navigate. However, my family and I arrived at our various destinations and returned back safely to our hotel every evening, rarely getting off track. How did we do that in a world with no knowledge? We found our way using a remarkable little invention called a map.

Did you ever think about what takes place when you use a map? Maps represent a belief about what a piece of the world is like (Washington, D.C., in my case). There is a simple way to test to see if that belief is correct. We find our current location on the map, plot a course, then move out. If our beliefs are true (if the map is accurate), we arrive where we intended to go. If our beliefs are not accurate, we'll learn that soon enough.

Notice that perfection is not required in this enterprise. Sometimes we get it wrong, but even then we know we're wrong because of new, accurate information that shows us our error.

This little exercise repeats itself thousands of times a day, every day of our lives in the countless details we encounter as we navigate our world. Our beliefs about reality are like that map. We constantly test them to see if they match up with the world. When they do, we know our beliefs are true.

Every time we use a map or take a medicine or drive a freeway or move from bedroom to bathroom in the middle of the night, we prove that at least parts of the story of reality can be known. If not—if we couldn't know certain important things that are actually true about the world—we'd be dead in a day.

Of course, using a map to get to the D.C. zoo is not the same as figuring out the meaning of the universe. But it ought to put to rest the concern that truth is out of our reach. And if we can know many of the little things (and we can), I don't see why we shouldn't be able to figure out some of the big things.

You can immediately see, though, why people who think there is no truth would never take the Christian Story seriously—at least, not as the kind of story it claims to be. If there really is no truth that matters (and that's the kind we've been talking about), then one story is as good as the next, and there are lots of other options that are easier and more appealing (in some ways) than the Christian Story.

So, the concern that there simply cannot be a true Story about reality is overrated. But there's a variation of this mistake I should warn you about.

It's simply not going to do any good dismissing our account of the world as "your truth" in favor of your own story called "my truth." Since believing something can't make it true (otherwise there'd be no difference between believe and make-believe), it makes no sense calling any belief a "truth" as if they were the same thing.

Confused talking leads to confused thinking. Some beliefs are true. Others are not. The difference matters. If a story is not accurate to reality, it's not any kind of truth at all, so it can never be *my* truth or *your* truth, even though we may believe it. It can only be our delusion, or our mistake, or our error, or whatever else you may want to call it. But it could never be our "truth." I hope that's clear.

This your-truth-my-truth move is just a less direct way of asserting there is no Story, only a bunch of individual stories with none any more reliable than the other, and we've already seen that this approach is not going to work.

If our Story is really true in the deep sense, then it ought to be obvious that other religion stories, taken as complete pictures of the world, are simply mistaken. This does not mean, of course, they are wrong at every point. That would be a foolish mistake for me to make. There are many individual things a religion might teach that are completely sound, as far as they go. I mean, rather, that if the Story is true, all other stories *taken as a whole* cannot be true as well. To say otherwise would also be a foolish mistake.

A man once told me I was probably one of those bigoted people who thought 90% of the world was wrong about their religion. I agreed with the 90% part, but I told him it had more to do with math than with bigotry.

Think about this. Some religions teach Jesus is the Son of God and others deny it. Fair enough. But is it not clear that somebody is right and somebody is wrong on that score? There is simply no getting around it.

The great monotheistic faiths understand God as a distinct, individual person, whereas some Eastern religions see God as the impersonal sum of everything all put together. Is it not clear that, if there is a God, both of these notions cannot be true about him at the same time? Clearly, massive numbers of people are mistaken on one side of this issue or the other.[1]

When anyone dies, they *might* go to heaven, or they *might* go to hell, or they *might* be reincarnated, or they *might* disappear into nothing at all. But even a child can see they cannot do them all at the same time. Multitudes—the majority even—must be mistaken. Again, that's not bigotry. It's simple math.

And notice, I am not wasting our time by splitting hairs about inconsequentials. No, I am speaking of the heart of things, the foundations, the deep structures, the most basic claims about reality that religions make.

So then, though it's the rage these days to say all religions are basically the same, it turns out not to be the case at all. What ought to strike us, rather, is how unlike each other they really are. When it comes to the most important things, each religion's picture of reality is quite different from the others' (that's what makes them *different* religions, after all). And those differences simply cannot be smoothed over by invoking, for example, naïve stories about blind men and elephants that do not really get to the heart of the matter.[2]

CHAPTER 4

Two Obstacles

CHRISTIANS HAVE A PROBLEM when they fail to understand their own Story. They are not able to answer the two objections most frequently raised about their beliefs. These two obstacles are so daunting for non-believers, they simply cannot take the Christian Story as anything more than an implausible tale, like yarns about unicorns, leprechauns, or North Pole elves. Here are the obstacles.

It is clear to most people that the world is not the way it ought to be. Something has gone terribly wrong, and everybody knows it. That's the first part of the first obstacle. The second part is this. If there were a God, and if he really were good, and if he really were powerful, then the world would be a different kind of place than the one we find.

A God who is both strong and good would prevent the mess we're in or, at least, would shield us so nothing harmful, difficult, or unpleasant would happen to us. This, I think, is a completely understandable impulse coming from a skeptic. If there really were a God, he would fix things or, more likely, would never let them get so bad in the first place.

Less understandable to me is that even Christians stumble over this same obstacle. They have been led to believe that if God were really a good God, and if they were truly good Christians, then they would be shielded from the hardships others endure, or (they may have been told) when hardships do come, Jesus would be their bridge over troubled waters, keeping them from harm. Instead, when they find themselves sinking in a flood of woes, they are caught by surprise. Then they wonder whether God was ever there to begin with.

Both confusions (the skeptic's and the Christian's) are based on a misunderstanding. As we will see, evil is not the problem for Christianity that people think it is because it is not foreign to the Story. It is central to it. It fits right in. In a certain sense, the entire Story is precisely about how the world went bad and how it gets fixed.

There is another misunderstanding I want to point out, something that seems never to occur to anyone regarding this first obstacle. First, note that the obstacle itself can be divided into two parts. The discovery that things are not right (first part) causes people to wonder if there really is a God (second part). The first part tells us about a problem. The second part tells us what people think they might properly *infer* from the problem. When the trains are running on schedule, it's likely because the person at the switchboard is doing his job. But when things consistently go awry, it's reasonable to ask if anyone is minding the controls at all.

What isn't obvious is that nothing is really solved by getting rid of God, though that is the standard move at this point. I say this because removing God from the equation, though understandable, does nothing to eliminate the problem that caused someone to doubt God's existence in the first place. God is gone, but the original problem remains. The world is still as broken. Atheism settles nothing on this matter.

What now is the atheist to do? Nothing has really changed. Things still are not the way they're supposed to be, so the atheist continues to be plagued with the same problem he started with. But given a Godless, physical universe, the idea that things are not as they should be makes little sense. How can something go wrong when there was no right way for it to be in the first place?

So first I am saying there is an obstacle raised by skeptics and Christians alike that is based largely on a misunderstanding about the problem of evil that I hope the unfolding Story will help resolve. And next I am saying that atheism—what at first seems like a reasonable response to the obstacle—ends up creating a serious problem of its own. When people do not understand how the Story deals with evil, they are going to stumble when they consider that issue.

They're going to stumble on another point as well. It is the second obstacle. That problem is tied to the question "If there is a heaven, how do I get there?"

To many, the Christian Story seems so narrow in light of today's sensibilities that it's almost suffocating. Only one way to heaven? That is nearly impossible for most people to take seriously. It's not only incredible; it borders on bigotry. As one bumper sticker states, "God is too big to fit into one religion," and those who think differently think too highly of themselves and their own beliefs. Does God really care about the details? After all, isn't he more interested in how a person behaves than in what he believes?

It might be helpful to note at this point that even though Christians are faulted for being small-minded and provincial in their view of a "tribal God who only cares for his own little group" (as one person put it), the "intolerant" narrow way was not an idea invented by them. The notion itself goes back to the ancient Hebrew prophets. It was, arguably, their chief concern for 1,500 years of the Story, captured notably in the first commandment God gave to his people.

In the Common Era, Christians promote the narrow view that Jesus is the only way precisely because Jesus himself was the author of it. He made the claim repeatedly, many times in many ways. Every disciple on record who was personally trained by Jesus to carry on after him delivered the same message: There is a narrow way to eternal life that few find; but a wide way to destruction that many follow. Indeed, *Christian* was not the label the followers of Jesus initially used of themselves. Rather, they called their group *the Way*, in light of Jesus' own claim.[1]

Of course, some will quickly note that just because Jesus taught it does not automatically make it true, and they would have a point. But it does seem to make the narrow view more difficult to dismiss. Jesus of Nazareth is a person most people are inclined to take seriously—which is why they freely quote him when it suits their purpose.

But why would Jesus, of all people, say such a thing? Wasn't Jesus' main message about equality, fairness, social justice, loving our neighbors—*inclusion*, in a word, not *exclusion*?

It is fashionable these days to presume such things about Jesus, but those were not the reasons he came—at least not the reasons *he* gave. Jesus cared about those issues, no question, which is why we find them scattered here and there within his teaching, but they were not the heart of it, not according to him.

No, there is a reason why Jesus made this controversial claim about himself, and it had nothing to do with arrogance, bigotry, or small-minded exclusion—a kind of cruel trick played on unsuspecting people to guarantee their damnation. Rather, it had to do with the drama itself and is, ironically, tied directly to the first obstacle—what went wrong with the world.

As it turns out, the brokenness of the world and the unique role of Jesus are connected. The second solves the first. That's a main point of the Story. It's one thing I hope you will see, that the two most controversial aspects of Christianity turn out to make complete sense once you understand the Story's big picture.

CHAPTER 5

Story Line

WHEN YOU LEARN A NEW LANGUAGE, you don't start at the beginning of the dictionary. You start with common objects and frequently used phrases. You start with the basics and then build upon them.

People wanting to learn about God sometimes start at the beginning of the Bible and read through to the end, expecting they will be able to separate the main things from the secondary things. They think this will make everything clear, but that method almost never works. A better approach is to start with the basic, foundational concepts and build on them. First, get the Story's basic outline in your mind and then go from there.

So let me give you the backbone—the plot line—of the Christian Story. It tells the most important things that happen in the order they take place and consists of five words: God, man, Jesus, cross, resurrection (here I mean the final resurrection at the very end of the Story). That's the big picture. It is both the storyline and the timeline, the beginning (God) to the end (resurrection).

Do you see the logical order of these five elements? Our story starts with God. He created everything from nothing, including the most valuable thing in all creation: man. But something went terribly wrong and human beings got themselves into a lot of trouble. So God initiated a rescue plan. He entered the world he created by becoming a human being, just like us—the man named Jesus. To rescue us from our problem, Jesus did something utterly unique that culminated on a cross. How people respond to what he did will determine what will happen to them at the final event of history, the resurrection.

Notice, you have all the parts of a good story: beginning, conflict, conflict resolution, ending. You also have all the pieces of a complete worldview: creation, fall, redemption, restoration.

The whole story takes hundreds and hundreds of pages to tell. It's probably the longest story ever written. But I'd like to tell you the basics of the Story quickly. In a sense, I want to show you the puzzle's cover—the big picture of the Christian worldview—so you never get lost in the details again.

I have said the Christian Story has been frequently misunderstood. But the basics are not that hard. You just have to start at the right place. You have to start at the beginning, with the foundation.

So now I want to tell you that Story. I want to give you the big picture of Christianity. I want to tell you the Story of Reality.

PART ONE

GOD

CHAPTER 6

In the Beginning

EVERY STORY HAS A BEGINNING. The first words of our Story go like this: "In the beginning, God created the heavens and the earth."[1] I think it's the second greatest line in the whole Story. I'll tell you later what I think the best line is.

I want you to notice a few important things about the Story from its start.

First, notice that it begins with a person, not a thing. That's because God existed before he made anything else, and he himself was never made. Before anything else was there, God was there. The universe is not eternal, but God is. He is an everlasting Spirit with no beginning and no end. He does not have a body like you and me. The Story does not start with gods, like some other stories, or with physical objects like the sun or the moon. It starts with one individual, infinite, perfect Person.

If you want to begin to teach your children (or anyone, for that matter) the Story, this is probably the best place to start. Start at the beginning. Start with the foundation. The foundation is God. He is responsible for everything that is. One ancient creed put it this way: "I believe in God, the creator of heaven and earth."

Our Story starts with a person for another reason. It's the next thing I want you to notice. God is the very first piece of the Christian Story because the Story is all about him. God is the central character. The Story does not start with us because the Story is not about us. When I was young my mother used to say, "Gregory, the world does not revolve around you." It was one of the most important lessons she could teach me. Your mother probably told you the same thing. Our mothers were right. We have an important part to play in the Story, but we are not the most important players.

Many people are confused on this point. When discouragement, disillusionment, or defeat creep into their lives, they are caught by surprise. They thought the Story was about them—their happiness, their comfort, their personal prosperity. Then they wonder what went wrong when things go in another direction. "How could God let this happen to me?" they ask. They thought that with God in their lives they would be the center of his attention and everything was going to be easier. Then they are caught off guard when things work out differently.

That's what happens when we think the Story is about us. In fact, a large part of the Story was written to people who believed in God and trusted in him yet experienced tremendous conflict and distress in this world. Suffering is standard fare in life, but especially so for those who take the Story seriously.[2] This is a clue that man did not make up the Story by himself. If he did, he probably would have written a different story.

There is a saying that has been helpful in some ways but I think is misleading in this regard. The saying goes, "God has a wonderful plan for your life." From what I understand now, that perspective is in the wrong order. The Story is not so much about God's plan for your life as it is about your life for God's plan. Let that sink in. God's purposes are central, not yours. Once you are completely clear on this fact, many things are going to change for you.

So the first two things I want you to see are that the Story starts with a person, and that's because the Story is about him, not us. Here is the third important detail to notice: In this Story, everything belongs to God.

The basic principle is a commonsense one: If you make it, it's yours. When someone invests labor and personal creativity to fashion something of value, then that valuable thing belongs to them and should not be taken from them. The way the Story puts it is this: It's wrong to steal. It's wrong to take something that is not yours. The concept of private property, then, is an important one in the Story; otherwise the command not to steal would make no sense.

Since God made everything out of nothing, it all belongs to him. He has proper authority to rule over all because none of it would exist without him. That includes you and me, by the way. We don't own ourselves—God does. Let that sink in too. When we claim absolute ownership over anything without the understanding that God holds the ultimate title, it's very much like stealing.

Here is why this last point is so important. Nowadays, when certain ethical issues come up, it's common to hear someone say, "I have a right to do whatever I want with my own body." It's a popular point, but it isn't quite accurate, is it? First, no one can do whatever he wants with his own body, not in a civilized society anyway. Second, if God made us, then our bodies are not our own, strictly speaking. We inhabit them, of course, and have an important connection with them. But if God is God, then we are not completely free to do as we wish with our bodies. In the end, the Potter has the right over his own clay.

"Does it not make a great difference," C. S. Lewis once observed, "whether I am, so to speak, the landlord of my own mind and body, or only a tenant, responsible to the real landlord? If somebody else made me, for his own purposes, then I shall have a lot of duties which I should not have if I simply belonged to myself."[3]

So, according to the Story, we belong to God because he made us. We don't own ourselves. But here I need to make a clarification. We belong to God, true enough, but not in the same way other things belong to him. We are not merely objects that are owned. We are human beings who are precious to God in the same way a child is precious to his parent. Yes, God is a great and powerful king. We must never lose sight of that. Indeed, to fear him is the beginning of wisdom. Yet he is also a Father.

In this story God made you to know him, to delight in him, to depend on him, to rest in his arms. Because you belong to God in this special way, you are not alone. There is a place for you—a safe place, a home—even if you haven't discovered that yet. No one is an orphan. We are his, and our hearts are restless until they find their rest in the home he provides, that is in himself.[4]

In this way the Christian Story is different from, for example, the Muslim story. The God of Islam is the supreme sovereign, to be sure. In that way these stories are similar. But Allah is not a father and humans are not his children. To a Muslim, that would be a blasphemous thing to think since, to them, it would diminish and, therefore, demean God.

In our story God is not far off, but near to us. He is a refuge, a shield, a fortress, a present help in time of trouble. He is not just the grand and splendid object of our awe. He is also the tender subject of our love.

Fourth, notice that in this story God is distinct from the rest of creation. This is an important point. Nature is not God. Rather, God made nature. The planet is not a person. That's a different story. In this story, the planet is a thing. The sun and moon are not beings to be worshiped. They do not have names. They have functions. They are things, not gods.

Strictly speaking, in this story you do not respect nature. Rather, you respect the Person who made nature by caring properly for what he has entrusted to you. You also respect the people you share nature with by not leaving an ugly mess that makes their world unpleasant or unsafe. It's a way of loving one's neighbor. But you do not respect nature. Treating a thing like a person is actually a form of idolatry.

The kingdom God made now consists of two different kinds of things: physical things you can touch or see, and nonphysical things you cannot experience with your senses but are still real.

The world is filled with these invisible things, and we encounter them all the time. Most of us never think about them much, though, because we perceive them in a different way than, say, the fragrance of turkey on Thanksgiving or Beethoven's *Fifth Symphony* or the cold nose of your pet schnauzer. Yet these invisible things are quite real and familiar to us. Think, for a moment, of your own thoughts. You know the thoughts you are thinking but not because you see, hear, touch, taste, or smell them. A different "sense" gives you access to them. Your thoughts are real and you know them, but they are not physical.[5]

In this story, then, there is a physical world and a nonphysical world.

Both are real. Material things (like birds and babies and asteroids and atoms) and immaterial things (like spirits and souls and minds and miracles) are equally at home. However, God is not nature and nature is not God. That is a different story.

Next I want you to see that the Story has a theme. This is pretty important since it gives meaning to the entire business of living. It provides a kind of end purpose or ultimate destination for everything. When people ask, "What is the meaning of everything?" or "What is the point of life?" or "What's it all about, anyway?" the Story's theme provides the answer. Without it, we would be hard-pressed to know what the "happily ever after" would look like in our story.

Did you ever wonder how to sum up the main theme of the Bible accurately in a single, simple concept? It's right there in the first line: "In the beginning, God created the heavens and the earth." Put simply, the Story starts with a Sovereign who creates a domain he benevolently rules over. There is a King and his "dom," so to speak. There is a *kingdom*.

This is what the Story is all about. The main theme is not love or redemption or forgiveness or even relationship. Those are all important parts of the Story, to be sure. They serve the theme in important ways, but they are not the main point of the Story. The idea that God owns everything and has proper authority to rule over everything he has made is the main point.

Here is another way of looking at it: The universe is managed by some *One*, not some *thing*. We are not abandoned to the fates or to the blind and brutal forces of the natural world. Instead, we have a powerful King carefully watching over us and who is there for us.

God is an active player in the Story. He does not sit silently and idly by. He is the storyteller, but he is also a player in the drama. He shows up. Because he is there, we are not alone. Because he speaks, we are not in the dark. Because he participates, we are not forsaken. More important than anything else, because he makes himself known, then we can know him.[6]

The Story calls this theme "the Kingdom of God" (or sometimes "the Kingdom of Heaven," but it means the same thing). You might even call it the "rulership of God" if you want to, since that's what the concept of kingdom amounts to. Only while under God's rulership can man fulfill his chief purpose—glorifying his King—and only under God's rule can man discover his deepest satisfaction—enjoying him forever.[7]

The kingdom theme is especially obvious later in the Story. A prophet named John comes preaching the Kingdom of God. He prepares the way for Jesus of Nazareth who also preaches the Kingdom of God. The disciples and apostles who follow after him preach the Kingdom of God. They preach that God is in charge, that the world belongs to him, and that coming back under his care and direction is the true secret to happiness. It is the only place where those who are weary and weighed down with life's woes will find true rest.[8] We do not just return to a sovereign, but, like the prodigal son, we come home to the protective care of a father. And because there is no limit to this sovereign's power, and because he is a noble, honorable, and perfectly worthy king, it's a good thing for us that he is the one who is in charge.

Now, I realize the idea that God is in charge is bothersome to many people, but what is the alternative? If someone is not in charge, then no one is in charge, and that seems to be a big part of our complaint about the world to begin with. Of course, it's entirely fair to raise the point that if someone is in charge, then why are things such a mess, but that is something we will get to later on. As I said before, the whole Story is about how God puts the world right again.

Think about this. Some homes are governed by a strong-willed child, or worse, a band of them. Chaos reigns because children do not know what is best for them. When they consistently get their way, mischief abounds. Generally, this is not a home where you want to spend much time.

Usually, though, the problem is not the strong-willed child, but the weak-willed parent. Thoughtful grownups know that no child really fares well in a home like that. Even though the youngsters think, for the moment at least, that life could not be better, that will not last. As one friend of mine used to say regarding children, "No pain now, big pain later."

When the whole world is run by children doing as they wish, ugly things happen. That's our complaint. Deep inside we hunger, like unruly children do, for things to be different, for someone bigger and trustworthy to be in charge so that good would prevail, even though, if we were honest, we'd have to admit that we (like the unruly children) are the main source of the problem. We need to be ruled if anything is going to be different.

There is a prayer in the Story that says, "Thy Kingdom come, Thy will be done, on earth as it is in Heaven." The petition is a wise one because it asks for something each of us desires deep in our heart—for goodness and justice to prevail in a world that lacks them. We are hungering for the thing we were made for. We are hungering for God's Kingdom.

One final thing. The world has not always been broken. That is not the way things started out. If it was, if the world now is the way it had been from the beginning, it would be difficult to imagine how it might be any different.

According to the Story, though, when God made everything, when he formed the world at the first and set up his Kingdom, everything was exactly the way his noble mind intended. Everything was in its proper place. Everything was fulfilling its designated purpose. This is the heart of happiness—all the world, and everything and everyone in it, working together in perfect harmony just the way God wanted it.

That isn't to say nothing could ever disrupt it, disorder it, throw it out of kilter. The happiness was not immutable. It could change. Things could go wrong. But they did not start out that way. They started out right. Everything was just the way it was supposed to be. Which is just another way of saying that everything God made was good.

CHAPTER 7

Two Objections

IT MIGHT BE HELPFUL at this point to pause and address two issues that come up a lot. Here's the first. It's pretty common, nowadays, to hear people ask the question, "Who created God?" I think it's an odd question, though. Children ask it frequently, but we expect it from them. Pretty much everything they encounter came from somewhere else, so it's natural for them to ask where God came from.

Adults, I think, should realize this is not a proper question. I have never met anyone (believer or nonbeliever) who thought that if God existed—at least the kind of God we're talking about—he would be the kind of being that needed to be created. That's why it strikes me as strange when these same people ask, "Who created God?" The question presumes that God was created, but no one believes that, certainly not Christians, so this is not a question any theist has to answer.

An eternal, self-existent Being has no beginning, so he needs no creator. This doesn't prove such a Being exists, of course. It only shows that those who believe in God do not have to answer inappropriate questions about his origin.

A related issue is this: "What *caused* God?" This is much like the first question, and it falters in a similar way since it is based on a similar misunderstanding.

Common sense tells us that anything that *happens* is always a result of some other thing that made it happen. If we had reason to believe that God popped into the world like scientists think the universe did, then "What caused God?" would be a proper question.

However, that is not what the Story teaches. God did not "happen" in that sense. He did not *come from* anything since he never *came to be* in the first place. Because the Story teaches God had no beginning (unlike the universe), but always was, there is no need to answer questions like this one either. That's why I say this question is based on a misunderstanding. Again, this doesn't prove the Story is right about God not having a beginning, but it does show that the question about his origin doesn't apply to a story like this one. It might be a good question to ask, though, of gods in other stories.

The second issue is a concern about miracles. I know the opening line of the Story ("In the beginning, God created the heavens and the earth") seems unbelievable to some, but there's good reason to believe something like this actually happened. Let me give you the best reason I can think of to believe that the first words of our story describe what really took place long, long ago before anyone was around to see it.

Consider this. Virtually no one who has thought about the issue at all—especially people like astrophysicists who spend their lives studying such things—believes the universe has always existed. Scientists pretty much agree that everything in the universe had a beginning. All physical things exploded into existence in a fraction of an instant long ago in what people call the Big Bang. The term started out as kind of a joke, but it stuck because it fit so well.

I know the Big Bang idea is controversial with some Christians, but I think that's because they haven't realized how well it fits the Story, which basically says the same thing. It doesn't say that everything came from nothing—which would be very hard to believe, I think, harder even than believing in God. That's because common experience—not to mention common sense—teaches that anything that happens is always a result of some other thing that made it happen, and nothing at all makes nothing at all happen. By contrast, what the Story says makes perfect sense. It says that everything came from some *One*.

What I'm going to say next may be an odd way of putting it, but it gets right to the point: A big bang needs a big banger. To most people that seems correct the moment they let it sink in. Once you realize how amazingly obvious that statement is, the idea that the some *thing* that caused the universe was actually some *One* becomes much more plausible. And it is a short logical step from there to the conclusion that this One, who would have existed before the time-space-physical world he created, is not bound up inside it or subject to it.

If God made everything out of nothing (unlike some other stories where gods made things from stuff that was already there), that means he's pretty powerful and pretty smart. What are the chances then, do you think, that he can change water into wine if he wanted to or make a blind man see or cause the sun to stand still for a day (as odd as that may sound)?

A simple principle is at work here. A person who's won an Olympic weightlifting medal probably could manage carrying your boxes up the stairs if you asked him. You see the point. If God created the entire universe in an instant (and we now know that could well be what happened), then just about anything else out of the ordinary would be pretty easy by comparison.

That's why in this story you'll find things happening that wouldn't make any sense at all in a world of a different sort—instant healings, massive bodies of water parting on command, loaves and fishes miraculously multiplied, even people coming back from the dead—yet they fit quite properly into our story. Here, the system is subject to its Master. The Maker controls the matter, not the other way around.

CHAPTER 8

Matter-Ism

SO ON THE CHRISTIAN VIEW, God and the world—mind and matter—are two different kinds of things. Both are real. The first (God) is maker and sovereign over the second (everything else). It's important to be clear on this in light of two competing stories you will encounter.

According to the first alternative, matter is all that exists. The only things that are real are physical things in motion governed by natural law. Though this view sounds very modern and up to date, it is actually quite old, going back thousands of years to the first people who began to wonder about such things.

The everything-is-matter story starts, "In the beginning were the particles." One famous person described it this way: "The cosmos is all that is, or ever was, or ever will be."[1] This is where the story starts, and this is where the story ends, because there is nothing more. No God. No souls. No heaven or hell. No miracles. No transcendent morality. Just molecules in motion following the patterns of natural law.

You might want to call this view "matter-ism," though most people call it "materialism." It's also called physicalism or naturalism because it involves physical stuff being pushed and pulled around by natural laws. These three words are not exactly synonyms, but using them that way is close enough for our discussion.

Of course, the matter-ism story is nothing like our story. This is a competing story of reality. It does have some of the same puzzle pieces as ours but leaves out so many other pieces that the final picture is radically different. This is the story that most atheists, most "skeptics," most humanists, and most Marxists believe is true. It's also the story that many non-atheists *act* like is true, even when they say they believe something else.

Many people think matter-ism is a reasonable thing to believe. That's because so much of what we are aware of is physical: everything we can see, everything we can touch, everything we can hear or taste or smell. It's one of our first and most powerful impressions of the way things are.

But isn't something missing?

When I said there is nothing more than matter in this story and this is where the story ends, I didn't mean there were no other details that were important to those who believe this account of reality. I meant that it's difficult to see how anything *deeply* meaningful can result. If at the end of the day the world is nothing but mindless matter in motion, then where does that leave us?[2]

Some thinkers committed to this view have been quite candid on this point. One put it this way: "It is already evident that all the objective phenomena of the history of life can be explained by purely naturalistic or materialistic factors. . . . Therefore, mankind is the result of a purposeless and natural process that did not have him in mind."[3]

This next one is a bit more colorful—coming from one of matter-ism's more colorful advocates, Richard Dawkins—yet it makes my point exactly:

> In a universe of blind physical forces and genetic replication, some people are going to get hurt, and other people are going to get lucky; and you won't find any rhyme or reason to it, nor any justice. The universe we observe has precisely the properties we should expect if there is at the bottom, no design, no purpose, no evil and no good. Nothing but blind pitiless indifference.[4]

Seventeenth-century philosopher Thomas Hobbes summed up this view famously, if indelicately, when he said that life in an unregulated state of nature is "solitary, poor, nasty, brutish, and short." Nature red in tooth and claw, that sort of thing. Or as one wit put it, "Nature has only one commandment, not ten—eat or be eaten."[5]

And they are right, it seems, if matter-ism is true. Many who hold this view, however—most, I dare say—have not felt the full force of it.

Here is one of the difficulties with matter-ism.

We all know that something has gone terribly wrong with the world. We call it "the problem of evil." But that can only be so if there is a right way for things to be. And that could only be so if the world was designed for a Purpose that for some reason is not being achieved. But it's hard to make sense of "Purpose" and "things gone wrong" if we are driven solely by "a purposeless and natural process that did not have [us] in mind," if there is "no design, no purpose, no evil and no good," and if life in the final analysis is nothing more than "solitary, poor, nasty, brutish, and short."

To be clear, in matter-ism there is no mind, no cosmic force, no plan, no Purpose. I've capitalized "Purpose" here since I am referring to an ultimate Purpose, a majestic Purpose, a Purpose beyond and above our mere personal projects.

Of course, anyone can come up with his or her own private, individual purpose that may be grand for them. But still, it could never rise to anything greater than self-interest (however noble their personal purpose may sound), since there is nothing greater than self-interest because in matter-ism no ultimate Purpose exists.

Remember too that when people get to make their own purposes, the door is opened to limitless variety, with no individual purpose better than any other. There would be no way to say, for example, that Megan the social worker could have a purpose that was any better than Robert the stockbroker or even (as ghastly as it sounds) Drake, the sex-slave trader, since that would require a Purpose that served as a kind of benchmark the others could be measured by. But in matter-ism that benchmark does not exist.

We should not be surprised, then, when those who take this view seriously—if they were brutally honest—are eventually overcome with a gnawing sense of futility. For to take this view to its logical and proper conclusion, in the final analysis life is ultimately empty, meaningless, purposeless, cold, and void. Philosophers call this "nihilism," which means "nothing-ism." And when someone starts really believing nothing-ism about themselves and other human beings, bad things begin to happen.

These are some of the reasons I do not think matter-ism, taken as a whole, is an adequate picture of reality.

CHAPTER 9

Mind-Ism

SO MATTER-ISM IS THE FIRST competing story. The second alternative is also an ancient one. In this view, Mind is all that exists—a Divine Mind (or, some might say, a "Divine Being"). This story starts, "In the beginning, Mind," and this is where the story ends too, because there is nothing more. When I say "there is nothing more," I mean that quite literally.

According to this story there is only one, single thing that is real—"God"—and God as Mind exists in a perfect, undivided unity. Here I don't mean what the Christian Story means by a personal God (that's why I just used the pronoun "it" to describe it). Rather, I mean a universal Mind permeates everything because it is the only thing. God is *in* everything—people, animals, nature, the cosmos—simply because he *is* everything.

Someone once called this view "pan-everythingism," a takeoff on the word "pantheism," which is a popular name for this view.[1] It's officially called "monism"—which actually means "one-ism"—but we can call it "Mind-ism" to help us remember that the one single thing that exists is Mind.

There are many variations of this view. Some schools of Hinduism and other Eastern religions promote this general picture of the world. If you are a student of those religions, you might have heard the everything-is-God view expressed by the phrases "All is One" or "*Brahman* [God] is *Atman* [self], and *Atman* is *Brahman*."

This picture of reality is also central to what has come to be called "New Age" (though it's actually not new at all). Environmentalism is sometimes implicitly an expression of the everything-is-God view, since pantheism has a tendency to deify nature.[2]

Because this story is such a popular one (folks in Hollywood seem especially attracted to it), it's important that you are clear on exactly what it involves.

First, we've already learned that in this story everything is God, including us. This idea has strong appeal because it initially makes us feel rather important. Note this dramatic statement taken from *The Secret*, a successful book of the New Age version of this view.

> You are God in a physical body. You are spirit in the flesh. You are Eternal Life expressing itself as you. You are a cosmic being. You are all power. You are all wisdom. You are all intelligence. You are perfection. You are magnificence. You are the creator, and you are creating the creation of You on this planet.[3]

Heady stuff. You probably didn't realize you were God in human form, but according to the Mind-ism story you are, kinda (I'll explain the "kinda" part in just a bit). The reason you don't realize you are God is because you have forgotten, so you need to be reminded in books like this one. Man is God who has temporarily forgotten, but can, when properly instructed, be restored to his full experience of divinity.

Second, we find our way back by choosing among many routes to enlightenment. Each individual is free to choose his own way, since just about any spiritual path, properly pursued, will eventually bring him to the ultimate destination—the liberation (*moksha*) of "you" (*Atman*) into immersion with the universal God (*Brahman*).

I say "eventually" because no one can expect to accomplish this task in one lifetime. It takes many lifetimes to arrive at enlightenment, which you might think of as Mind-ism's equivalent of heaven, since it is the final destination of ultimate bliss. It wouldn't do to call it that, though, since the *state* of enlightenment is so completely different from the *place* we call heaven it would be misleading.

Because every birth is a rebirth, everyone is "born again," in a sense, countless times. The self (in some form) takes on a new body again and again for many thousands of incarnations (technically, "re-incarnations") until the *Atman* finally works off its *karma* (the consequences of past actions) and disappears into the Divine the way a drop of water disappears into the ocean.[4]

The inherent flexibility of Mind-ism—many paths will lead you to the top of this mountain—is appealing to those who are put off by more "narrow" religions, particularly Christianity. It appears, at first glance, to be refreshingly open-minded.

Do not be misled by appearances, though. Every view of reality— including Mind-ism—is narrow in a fundamental way. There's no escaping it since the everything-is-God view, like every religion, offers a precise picture of reality that (taken as a whole) rules out all competitors (taken as a whole). If Mind-ism's claims about the world are accurate, then others' claims are not. If, for example, Mind-ism is true, then Jesus is wrong on just about everything. So was Mohammed. So was Moses. Again, no bigotry here, just simple math.

But now we come to a fork in the road, because the view that everything is God can take you in two slightly different directions. Classical Hinduism leads one way, and the New Age takes you in another.

In some versions of Hinduism you are God, true enough, but in a very real sense, you are no longer *you* anymore (that's why a moment ago I said you were "God in human form . . . kinda"). Things are not as they appear. To be more precise, the things that do appear aren't even things at all. Only *the one thing*, the impersonal God, is real. All else is an illusion called *maya*.

If this seems hard to imagine, think of it like this. At night when you drift off to sleep, the individual images that dance in your head—the people, the places, the objects, the events of your dreams—are not separate bits and pieces of a world *outside* you, but rather projections of your own imagination that remain *inside* your own mind. Of course, sometimes in the middle of a dream it seems quite real, but when you wake up you know better.

In Mind-ism, this is what the world is like—a kind of dream in the mind of God. This may not be a perfect analogy, but I think it gives you the general idea. The only real thing is God; the rest is just imagination. Once we "wake up" and are enlightened, the teaching goes, we see this.

Any appearance of being distinct, individual, and separate from God is a deceptive illusion.

At this point you might be feeling a little cheated, and I think I understand why. All of this talk about each of us being God—as attractive as that sounded at first—is now starting to look a bit empty.

Since all is God, then you are God too, but so are all manner of beasts revered or worshiped as divine—cows in India (famously), snakes, even insects for some. All is one and one is all. Everything is *equally* God and everything is *only* God because (as odd as this may sound) no thing is the thing it appears to be. That's the illusion. Or to put it more bluntly—and more painfully—*you* are the illusion.

Remember, in Mind-ism, God is an undivided *unity*—oneness. In the final analysis, there are no individual *things*. And if that's true, then anything that seems particular and individual is an illusion (*maya*), even you. That is why the initial sense of significance loses its luster when you realize what is actually being taught.

There is, however, a more optimistic—and therefore more appealing—option. In New Age thinking, the individual is not nothing; he is everything.[5] Note how the author of *The Secret* celebrates our common divinity at the close of the book.

> The earth turns on its orbit for You. The oceans ebb and flow for You. The birds sing for You. The sun rises and it sets for You. The stars come out for You. Every beautiful thing you see, every wondrous thing you experience, is all there, for You. Take a look around. None of it can exist, without You. No matter who you thought you were, now you know the Truth of Who You Really Are. You are the master of the Universe. You are the heir to the Kingdom. You are the perfection of Life. And now you know The Secret.[6]

Master of the Universe? Heir to the Kingdom? The perfection of life? Yes, this is much better, certainly an improvement on classical Hinduism's demotion to delusion. I think it's becoming obvious why so many Americans prefer this option. High on individual freedom and personal self-esteem (again, you are God, after all). Low on personal responsibility since God (you) answers to no one. What could be more liberating?

New Age Mind-ism is the ultimate "spiritual, but not religious" option, promising a kind of mystical piety at bargain prices with no inconvenient Deity looking over your shoulder spoiling the party—or as C. S. Lewis put it, "All the thrills of religion and none of the cost."[7]

Divinity comes at a price, though, one you may not have expected. Since (according to this view) you are the master of your own fate, then any ill that befalls you—any anguish, any disaster, any tragedy of any sort—is no one's fault but your own. You are responsible for your own reality (you are God, after all). There is no one above you whom you must answer to, true enough. But there is also no one above you to turn to when life goes south. There is no one greater than you to whom you can appeal because there is no one but you. You are in charge, but you are alone and completely on your own. That is the price you pay for being God.

There is something else tricky about the New Age version of Mind-ism that many miss. It was so surprising and troubling to me when I discovered it, I wanted to warn you in advance.

Listening to the teachers of this view and reading their writings, you will notice lots of words and phrases that will be familiar to you if you are a Christian. These authors regularly refer to "the Christ," "the Kingdom of God within you," "eternal life," "the way, the truth, and the life," the "I am"—that sort of thing. And you'll hear many references to Jesus and lots of quotes from the Bible.

Here's the amazing part. Some have suggested that the New Age story is the way the Christian Story really goes, but Christians have misunderstood it. Jesus himself, they say, was a New Age guru whom we mistook for a Torah-observant Hebrew prophet when he was really a Hindu all along.

Now here's the warning. The New Age story is not the Christian Story. It is a completely different picture of reality that sometimes has Christian pieces mixed in that are then force-fit to make them appear as if they belong. As a result, many who think themselves Christian end up in the New Age story by accident without realizing it. This happens because they do not fully understand the Christian Story.

So, to eliminate any confusion on this point, I am going to give you a short quiz. In the Christian Story, who is the creator and sustainer of the universe? Who is the Lord, the master of the universe? Who is all powerful? Who is the center of the universe? The answer to each of these questions is, of course, God—the God who is completely distinct from the rest of his creation.

By contrast, in the New Age story of reality, who is the creator and sustainer of the universe? Who is the Lord, the master of the universe? Who is the all-powerful one? The New Age answer is, you are. That's why you are also the center of the universe.

Can you see the dramatic difference between the New Age story and the Christian Story I have been telling you? They are different stories. Indeed, they are opposites in critical ways. Yes, the New Age story uses pieces of the Christian puzzle, but this is misleading. The New Age Mind-ism picture of reality—the final story it tells—is entirely different from Christianity.

In our story, God made the world and we are his subjects. This makes some people uncomfortable. I understand that. It also makes the Mind-ism story attractive since God is the same as the world—meaning you are *part* of God—and in one version of this view you *are* the "God" who is continuing to make your own world. But a story being attractive and a story being true are two entirely different things. Never forget that.

I can sum up Mind-ism this way. Either self is nothing, or self is everything (God).

So, what do you think of the Mind-ism view? I'm not asking whether you like it or not, because there are many things we like that are not, in the long run, either good or true. Asking what you like would be fine if you were dining out or decorating your home or naming your cocker spaniel. When it comes to the true-story-of-reality issue, though, we must set aside our preferences and ask different questions.

This is something you must be clear on. I'm not asking you what you *feel*. I'm asking you what you *think*. For that, you must put your thinking cap on for a moment.

If the true story starts with Mind and ends with Mind, if nothing else actually exists, if there are no distinctions of any kind because Mind—or Being, if you will—is perfect unity, what follows? What else must you conclude about the world if you are thinking carefully?

Here it is: There cannot be a problem of evil, even in principle. As odd as it may seem, there is nothing wrong with the way things are. Everything just is. All-that-is is perfect at every moment. Or as one famous proponent of this view put it, "All is as it should be."[8]

How could it be otherwise? There can only be something terribly wrong with the world if there is a difference between terribly wrong and perfectly right in the first place. Yet in Mind-ism even morality is *maya*, illusion.

And if good and bad are illusions, then what becomes of forgiveness or mercy or grace or even love? All are casualties. The demands of *karma* are inflexible and unalterable. All creatures must get what they deserve. Every "sin" must be suffered for, and the suffering we experience is the suffering we deserve. And even this is *maya* in the long run.

Does that seem right to you? Does it seem like the world is just as it should be, all the time? Or does it seem like something has gone terribly wrong, and the world—and the people in the world, you and I—are terribly broken in some profound way?

This, I think, is the single biggest difficulty with taking Mind-ism seriously. It's the same as the biggest difficulty with taking matter-ism seriously. Neither can make any sense of mankind's most pressing problem, the problem of evil.

I think you can see why I do not think any form of the Mind-ism story is an adequate one. Put simply, I have good reason to think it false—it does not seem to fit the way the world actually is (broken and beleaguered)—and no good reason to think it true. Those are two pretty strong marks against it.

CHAPTER 10

Options

THERE ARE THREE MAIN ANSWERS to the question "Why are we here?" Maybe the easiest way to think about our options is this. First, there is some *One* behind it all (God-ism), a personal Mind who created and rightfully governs a world of material and immaterial things, including other minds. Second, there is some *thing* behind it all (Mind-ism) in which material and immaterial things, including other minds, are all illusions. Third, there is *no one* and *no thing* behind it all (matter-ism), just a material universe of physical things with no other minds and no invisible, immaterial things at all complicating the equation.

Which story do you think makes the most sense? Here is the significant clue I mentioned before that I do not want you to miss.

I said earlier that almost everyone agrees the world is not the way it ought to be. It should be a lot better than it is. But when you think about it, that's a very odd thing to believe if you also believe in matter-ism because it presumes there's a Purpose that is not being realized. Yet Purpose is the very thing that's impossible in a world filled only with matter. That does not ring true.

Evil is also a puzzle piece impossible to fit into a world filled with only a solitary Mind, because Mind is not merely center stage, it is the whole stage. Since in Mind-ism there is only a single, perfect, undivided unity, then any ultimate distinctions—even distinctions between good and evil—turn out to be illusions. Instead of the world being not quite right, in Mind-ism everything is already just as it ought to be all the time. But that does not ring true either.

Neither Matter-ism nor Mind-ism answers our deep concern about the world not being right. Worse, the question doesn't even make sense in those stories. In neither story (if we are to be consistent with their principles) can the matter be raised. But in real life the problem comes up all the time. That is the difficulty.

So, the first piece of our puzzle is God. The Story is about him, the Creator of everything else from nothing else. He is the rightful ruler over all he has made—his Kingdom. You and I are his lawful subjects. We are also his precious possession, made for friendship with him.

Since God creates with noble intention, there is a purpose—a proper goal—for everything and everyone. All that God made, and every way God made it, was just the way it was supposed to be. He is the author of the good, the true, and the beautiful, and is the most marvelous Being we could ever imagine. None is greater or more noble or more virtuous or more wonderful.

He is good, but he is not safe.[1] We must never forget that. Absolute goodness makes God absolutely dangerous, for the only ones who are safe are the ones who are good like he is.

PART TWO

MAN

CHAPTER 11

Beautiful

NOW IT'S TIME TO INTRODUCE YOU to another character in our story. He's next because he's the most important person after God. An entire chapter in the Story is devoted just to the creation of man.

There are two things you must never forget when you think about man. When we consider humans and the condition we are in, two things immediately become obvious: Man is very much like everything else in the created world in one way, but he is completely unlike anything else in the created world in another way.[1]

On the one hand, man, like everything else in the visible universe, is made of physical stuff. He has a physical body, which means he is a creature with limitations. This is what philosophers mean when they say man is "contingent." They mean humans are dependent on other things for their existence, their survival, and their well-being.

Put another way, humans are not little gods, and I need to state this forcefully because I do not want anyone to be confused on this point. In the Story, we did not begin as supernatural beings, and we will not end as supernatural beings. There is nothing magical or miraculous about us or our abilities. We are creatures from the beginning and will always be creatures. We are not the center of the universe. We are not God in physical bodies. We are not all power or all wisdom or all intelligence. Instead, we depend on and owe our existence to the God who made us from the dust, who sustains us at every moment, and who will return our mortal bodies to the dust when we breathe our final breaths. Let us never forget that we are creatures.

This does not mean we are not special, though. We are, in fact, the most wonderful creatures in the world next to God. It just means we should be careful, as the Story says, not to "worship and serve created things rather than the Creator."[2] Thinking of ourselves as divine is just another way of making the Story about us. There is a God, and we are not him, and pushing him off of his throne and taking it for ourselves is foolish. It is also dangerous.

No, we are not little gods, but we are not junk either. This is another mistake people make. They go from one extreme to another. They think that if we are not gods, then we must be nothing—cogs in the wheels, pieces of the machine of the universe and nothing more.

But there is more. So let me point out one other detail of our creaturely side that in itself is not especially remarkable but leads to the reason we are completely unlike anything else in the created world.

There is more to us than our physical bodies. We are made of physical stuff, of course, but we are made of nonphysical stuff too, an invisible self, a soul. This is obvious, it seems to me, and obvious to most people who have thought about it much. Many, however, especially those committed to matter-ism, deny that souls are real. Denying that humans are more than physical bodies is one reason why that view leads to the nihilism, the "nothing-ism," I mentioned earlier. And if we are just mechanical parts in a vast machine that has no purpose but just *is*, I can see their point. In our Story, though, man is not a machine but a human body in union with a human soul that gives life and motion and direction to his physical body.

Our souls, however, are not in themselves what make us different from other created things, since all sentient creatures—anything that is conscious or aware or thinks or feels—have souls too. This may surprise you, but that is what the Story teaches[3] and what believers in the Story have believed for thousands of years. No, it is not *having* souls that distinguishes humans from animals. What makes us special is *the kind* of souls we have.

But now I'm getting ahead of myself. First, I want to tell you something about man you already know but may not have thought about much because, like many things that are really obvious, it is easy to overlook. It is central to our Story. It's also so basic to being human that any story of reality that claims to be accurate must account for it. Here it is: Man as man—man as he was from the beginning, man as he is in himself, man in his essential nature—is wonderful. There is a certain beauty about being human that sets man apart from everything else.

Beauty, I think, is a good word to describe what I'm getting at, but it can also be misunderstood. Here I do not mean beautiful like a sunset is beautiful or a work of art or a Miss America or anything else like that. I am not talking about aesthetics, glamor, "good looks," or anything on the outside that can be seen with the eyes. I am also not talking about anything on the inside, if by *inside* you mean what people mean when they say, "She is such a beautiful person" or "Inner beauty is more important than outer beauty" or that kind of thing.

I am not talking about anything models or movie stars or Mother Teresa have and others do not have, or anything physical or anything any particular human does, or any personal virtues an individual possesses. I am talking about what human beings are at their core regardless of how they look, what they do, or what good or bad qualities they possess. I am talking about something true of all people who ever lived simply because they are humans and for no other reason, no matter how good or bad they are or how attractive or misshapen or small or smart or young or old—even so young or so old or so feeble or broken they are of no use to us or even to themselves. I am not talking about anything applied to the outside of the human "vessel," so to speak, or contained on the inside either, but rather something that is part of the vessel itself—not something attached to, but something built in.

Let me offer a crude analogy. (I say "crude" only because human worth can never properly be compared to the worth of any physical thing.) Gold has a certain value that follows it wherever it goes. Gold's value is, shall we say, in itself. It is intrinsic to gold, part of what gold is no matter what shape the gold takes.

The value I'm talking about in humans is like that. Man's value is in itself (or, better, in its *self*). We do not gain this value along the way, and we cannot lose it along the way either. Instead, the worth you and I have is built right in. It is with us from the first instant of our beginning and follows us wherever we go, no matter what "shape" we take. It will always be ours. Some essential part of you and me will always be wonderful and beautiful, and nothing and no one can take it away.

There are two reasons why I've labored here to make clear the particular way humans are special. First, our innate, built-in human value is the only reason we have any binding duties or obligations toward each other that we do not have toward any other kind of things. Of course, any person or any culture can simply make up some "duties" or "obligations" just like they can make up "purpose" for themselves, but that is not what I'm talking about here. I'm talking about something above mere human choice that does not change because it cannot change.

No rules that man invents by himself can ever be binding in any final or ultimate sense, since the person who makes the rules can simply change them whenever it suits his fancy or whenever the old rules get bothersome. But if there are obligations based on something changeless—for example, man's built-in value—then our obligations toward man cannot change either. Our duties to each other are not only above man's mere choice; they rule over his choices.

Second, man's special value is the only reason we have unalienable human rights. Unalienable rights are those that can never be taken away since the reason for our rights—the unique beauty of man—is always part of each one of us. They are unable to be taken away and they cannot be given away either, because they cannot be separated from our own selves.

I do not want you to miss the simple arithmetic here: If man's special value falls, then unalienable human rights fall, too. If man is not special, if he is not deeply different from any other thing, then there is no good reason not to treat him just like any other thing when it's convenient for us to do so. If man is just "the result of a purposeless and natural process that did not have him in mind," as matter-ism dictates, if he is just a gear in the machine, or if he is only an illusion of the universal Mind, then there is no good reason for unique and unalienable human rights.

It should not be surprising, then, when cultures consistently believe that there is nothing special about being human, that soon they deny ultimate moral obligations and unalienable human rights too. When man is reduced to a mere animal—when the force of one's worldview logic demotes humans to mere biological machines—morality and human rights die and power is all that remains. This has happened with every communist regime, and happens with all governments as they get increasing secular. It cannot be otherwise.

I said earlier we all know man is special. Yes, the beauty of man is built into us, but so is the knowledge of that beauty. It is a truth that is "self-evident," as the American founders put it, a truth clear to reasonable people when they reflect carefully on it.

We can tell we all know this by the way we talk about things. There are countless examples of this, but here is an obvious one. We tell our children not to act like beasts, and we are appalled when humans are treated like animals. Why? There is a reason it's okay to gas termites but not Jews. It's because we know people are different from other creatures in an important and wonderful way.[4]

It is also why, by the way, claiming that some questionable behaviors are "natural" for certain people (as many have done lately) is not enough to let them off the hook morally, since all sorts of sordid behavior turns out to be just fine if we followed that rule. Does a natural desire for food justify grocery theft? Does a natural hunger for sex nullify restraints to passion? Does a natural tendency toward violence (yes, some have claimed this) justify attacks on annoying people? Are humans not obliged to a higher law than the law of nature? Animals do what comes naturally. Humans should not.

The Story says we are not mere beasts. Yes, we are creatures, but we are more than creatures. We are human beings with animal appetites that would tyrannize us if not restrained by higher law. The difference between "just doing what comes naturally" and principled self-restraint is called civilization.

So, man has value that is not added on in some way but is built in, so to speak, intrinsic to being human. And this is something we already know because the knowledge of our value is built in too. Here we come to the core question about our innate dignity. Why are human beings, of all creatures, this way? Why is man so different from everything else? It's all well and good to believe you are special, but if there is no good reason to think you are, you might be tempted to believe people are actually mere animals after all—and that leads to nothing but trouble.

This is where the Christian Story stands out dramatically from all the rest.[5] The Story answers the question "Why?" It tells us why man is different, why humans are special, why you and I are wonderful in a way that can never change. It tells us that in all the world, God created only one creature who was, in a unique and important and almost indescribable way, like himself, bearing his own likeness, having a soul imprinted with his very image.

If you have ever asked yourself the question "Who am I?" you now have your answer. The Story says you are a creature, but you are not just a creature. You are not a little god, but you are not nothing. You are made like God in a magnificent way that can never be taken from you. No matter how young or old or small or disfigured or destitute or dependent, you are still a beautiful creature. You bear the mark of God. He has made you like himself, and that changes everything.

Two changes are especially important. First, because the image of God imprints value deep in our souls, it makes us worth protecting. Whether our bodies are deformed or misshapen. Whether we are feeble, drooling, bedwetting, old people in the twilight of our years. Whether we are little babies hidden away in our mothers' wombs or the smallest embryonic human beings about to be sacrificed for research. We are still valuable. We are made in the image of God.

This is the reason those who believed the Story rescued and adopted abandoned infants in the first century. This is why Christians fought to abolish slavery in the nineteenth century. This is the reason followers of Jesus help rescue sex slaves in the twenty-first century. It is also why our forebears fought the American Revolution and the Civil War and why there is a Bill of Rights. Here is how the Founders put it:

> We hold these truths to be self evident, that all men are created equal, that they are endowed by their Creator with certain unalienable Rights, that among these are Life, Liberty and the pursuit of Happiness.

I hope when you read those words you see something many people miss, a version of the arithmetic I mentioned earlier. The Founders did not simply fabricate human rights out of thin air, as many do today. They did not make up entitlements according to their whims. They were not inventing; they were observing. They saw something obvious ("self evident") about human beings, and they understood *why* humans were that way.

Human beings were *created* equal. God *made* man wonderful. We have been *endowed* by our Creator with certain rights. Man's dignity was built in, not simply added on. Note that if you remove the reason for the rights, you remove the rights too. If you remove the Creator, you remove the privileges he alone can give.

And if you are tempted to think that man in himself is sufficient for the task of endowing rights, always remember: Whatever rights man alone gives, man alone can take away. No, only the image of God in man can give us absolute value, ultimate purpose, and deep worth.

Second, God's imprint makes it possible for us to have a friendship with God. This is not a friendship of equals, to be sure. My daughters and I are friends, but we are not peers. In the same way, God is still King. He is still our Sovereign. That will never change. But he can also be our friend. Our King is not distant like a royal, but close like a father. This is what people mean when they say they have a "relationship" with God. It is the kind of friendship he intended from the beginning. It is what we were made for.

God made a wonderful garden for Adam and Eve to live in and gave them meaningful work to do. They were given charge over the world that God made for them and over all the creatures that lived in the world—not to dominate in a cruel and thoughtless way but to care for them so man would be fruitful and flourish. Creation was meant to be under man's hand, not under his heel.

God gave us everything we needed to be happy—that is, fulfilled, satisfied, living out all of God's good purpose. But the most important thing God gave was himself, that we be continually filled with joy in his presence and find sweet contentment in his provision.[6]

CHAPTER 12

Broken

NOW WE MUST TALK ABOUT another way humans are special. It is not anything attractive or wonderful though. It is something dark, disturbing, and sinister. Probably the simplest way to say it is this: Even though man is beautiful, he is also broken. Yes, man is noble, but he is also cruel.[1]

These two facts about human beings are so obvious that any view of the world—if it means to describe the world as it actually is—must account for them. And it must do so in a way that makes good common sense.

Most attempts to explain the world that are popular nowadays do not, it seems to me, do the job. One school of thought says man's real problem is that society has failed him in some way. People are bad because they are uneducated, and if they were just instructed properly they would be a lot nicer to each other or would not do stupid things that get them into trouble. Or folks falter because they are poor. Poverty causes crime, and if wealth were spread around a bit more evenly, then people wouldn't take things that did not belong to them. Eliminate ignorance and poverty (they say), and crime would pretty much be eliminated too.

These are both popular options of late, but I think you know this is just nonsense. Look around you. The rich and educated may not get caught as often, but they are no more noble than the ignorant and the poor.

Improving education provides opportunity for economic improvement, but it does not make people better. It has just produced more literate and, therefore, more clever criminals. In tough times like recessions and depressions, it turns out, crime rates frequently *drop*. Then they rise as people prosper.

No, ignorance and poverty are not the problem. Neither education nor economics gets to the real root of man's woes.

Another option is to say that man is not actually bad at all because nothing is really bad in any ultimate sense, that is, in the sense of breaking some kind of Law-over-everything-and-everyone. There is no grand Law of that sort, in this view, because once you begin talking about a Law like that, the notion of a Lawmaker-over-everything-and-everyone begins to creep into the conversation too, and that won't do for some people.

Instead, they offer two strategies to explain (or, rather, explain away) man's badness that require no inconvenient and unwelcome Lawmaker. The first says that what we call "right" and "wrong" merely reflects what civilized people have tacitly agreed on, for the moment, to help us all get along. The "for the moment" part is important, since these rules change from time to time and from culture to culture. What was vice for us in the past may be virtue in the future, and what is "bad" for our own culture may be "good" for another. Morality is all the group and only the group, and that's all anyone can say about good and bad since there is nothing higher than the group. Who's to judge? One man's terrorist is another man's freedom fighter, after all.

Now, there may be some limited truth to this idea, but it cannot be the whole answer. You have probably already guessed some of the problems with this explanation. For one, if the group is "right" by definition, and anyone who breaks ranks with the crowd is, therefore, on the "bad" side, then what will we do with a Mahatma Gandhi or a Martin Luther King Jr.? Social reformers always oppose the group, since if the mainstream were in the right to begin with, there would be no need for reform. This view also means that thugs like Nazis are, oddly, off the hook since they had their own social contract of sorts. It is a strange moral formula that brands Gandhi and King villains and exonerates the Third Reich, but that's what we are stuck with in this system.[2]

No, this explanation will not do. It seems obvious that the majority is not always moral. And furthermore, what rule *outside* the social contract obliges anyone to obey the contract in the first place? Is there not some kind of Law-over-everything-and-everyone necessary to make any such agreement workable to begin with?

The second strategy used to avoid anything like an "absolute" morality judging man's condition is the Darwinian one, very popular now with the matter-ism crowd. It reduces human behavior to natural patterns explained by evolution. According to this view, we have evolved convictions about right and wrong that we think are ultimate because they serve an evolutionary purpose.[3] We have been tricked by nature to talk about "good people" or "bad people" as if people really were good or bad, when all along morality is just a ruse to help us successfully get our "selfish genes" (as Richard Dawkins would put it) into the next generation. *Good*, then, is simply a euphemism for "biologically adaptive" or "reproductively successful" or something like that, and *bad* is just the opposite, more or less.

Yet once again, this cannot be the whole story even if (as some might argue) the Darwinian account tells us part of it. Lions are lions, which means they hunt down less able (and less fortunate) creatures, drag them to the ground, and devour them as they die. And though it is a ghastly thing to watch, how can we expect them to be any different? Lions are doing exactly what lions do. They are neither noble nor cruel. They are animals. The strong prey on the weak. It is in their nature, and we do not fault them for it. That is nature's way.

When it comes to man, though, we do expect something different and we fault him when it is not. But why? If the Darwinian idea is the correct one, then everything surviving is just "right" the way it is, perfectly adapted for this moment in biological history, nothing more, nothing less. There is no better or worse, no beautiful or broken. There are only survivors who are fit or casualties who are not.

No, these attempts to explain what makes man special will never work, simply because the kind of human beauty and human brokenness we are all innately aware of are not *quantity* differences at all (*level* of education, *amount* of income, *content* of social contract, *degree* of evolutionary adaptation), but *quality* differences—differences in value and worth, not differences in amounts. Yet this is exactly the kind of distinction that matter-ism cannot make, since value distinctions are not physical in themselves, though they may be about something physical.

So we are back to where we started. Man is beautiful, but man is broken. There simply is no getting around it. Something has gone deeply wrong with us, and the problem is not in our education or in our pocketbooks or in our cultural contract or in our genes. We are not the victims. We are the victimizers. The evil in the world is not out there. It is in us. Put simply, we are guilty, and we know it.

Chesterton famously pointed out that original sin (the brokenness I am talking about) is the one doctrine of Christianity that can actually be proven.[4] And I think *sin* is the right word here, though it has fallen from favor in recent times. It is always more convenient to point the finger elsewhere—at our environment, at our biology, at others, at God. But the fact remains—and when we are honest with ourselves we admit it—the brokenness in the world starts with the brokenness in us.

None of us can long avoid the gnawing sense of guilt we feel for the bad things we have done. This is a good thing, of course, for a couple of reasons. For one, the person who never feels bad about doing bad things (an especially unpleasant kind of person known as a sociopath) is not likely to stop himself from doing something dreadful when it suits him.

But there is another reason. It is a very small step from feeling guilty to realizing that we feel guilty because we are guilty.[5] And that is precisely what the Story tells us. We are broken, true enough. But we are not simply malfunctioning. We are not machines that need to be fixed. We are transgressors who need to be forgiven. We have not merely "made mistakes," like getting our sums wrong when balancing accounts. We have sinned. And with sin comes guilt. And with guilt comes punishment. The sin must be answered for. It must be paid for in some way. Atoned for, if you will.

So here is our question: Before whom do we stand guilty? To whom are we beholden? From whom do we need forgiveness?

Some try to settle, at this point, for "forgiving ourselves." It's a popular approach these days, but it makes no sense to me. Since I have not sinned against myself (whatever that means), I cannot be the source of my own pardon. Letting myself off the hook might make me feel better for a moment, but it will not do in the long run since I do not need relief from the *feeling* of guilt, but *from the guilt itself*, regardless of how I feel.

No, "forgiving ourselves" will not fix the brokenness. Absolution must come from somewhere else. It must come from the one we have wronged, the greater One, the One responsible for the Law-over-everything-and-everyone that we have broken. We are not beholden merely to a regulation but to the Person behind the regulation—our rightful Sovereign, God. Forgiveness must come from him, since he is the One we have sinned against.

Now, all this talk of sin and guilt and punishment is discomfiting, I understand. It is natural to look for some way out, to find some excuse, some way to minimize the complaint. And that is precisely what guilty people always try to do. "Nobody's perfect," we say. "We've all 'blown it' in some way." "To err is human." "I'm no Hitler, at least." And a host of other bromides meant to persuade ourselves we really are not so bad after all. But the situation is much worse than that, isn't it?

As to not being a Hitler, I am glad to hear it. One was bad enough. But that is hardly helpful since Hitler is not the standard. I suspect you are no Jesus either, and you are probably more like Hitler than you are like Christ.

To sharpen my point, let me ask you a few questions. Have you ever placed anything before or above God in your life? Have you ever disobeyed or otherwise dishonored your parents? Have you ever deceived someone or misrepresented the truth in any way? Have you ever taken something that was not yours or craved what belonged to another even if you didn't actually take it? Have you ever been sexually intimate with someone who was not, at the time, your spouse, and if not, have you ever even toyed with the idea in your mind?[6]

You see what I am doing, of course. I am holding your life (and mine) up to the only standard that matters, the one our lives will be tested against at the end. I am walking you through the most basic Commandments in the Story. There are ten of them, though these are just the beginning. There are many more.

Some think Jesus lightened our load by reducing our obligations down to two main ones, the so-called "Great" commandments. In reality, he increased the burden. First, he said, we must love God with every ounce of our being. Second, we must love even our worst enemy with the same force and passion that we love ourselves.[7]

So how are you faring? Not well, I suspect. No one does when their lives are compared closely to what is actually required. It is like looking in a mirror that reveals exactly what we are like. If we look at each other, we can always find someone nastier than ourselves. It is a false comfort, though, since we will not be judged by how someone else behaved. When we are forced to look at the true standard, we are not able to fool ourselves.

Have we kept all the commandments? Have our actions all been good ones? Have our motives all been true? Has there been a single moment in any of our lives when we have loved God with the intensity he deserves or loved our enemies as we have loved ourselves? There has not been for me. When measured by the true standard, are we not all found wanting? Are we not all grievous criminals before God every waking moment of our lives? Are you beginning to see just how bad things really are for us? Are you willing to admit just how deeply broken and profoundly guilty you truly are?

And take no comfort in hoping that somehow your good will outweigh your bad. This is not how law works. Laws are meant to be kept, and a violation of just one means trouble, even if we keep the rest. And we have not violated just one. We've broken them all, in many ways, many times over.

This means, of course, that our real problem is moral. Badness is the problem with the world, our badness. And here we come to a critical point in the Story: The thing that went wrong with man caused what went wrong with the world. The world is broken because we are broken. Our badness made the world go bad.

CHAPTER 13

Lost

WE HAVE BEEN CONSIDERING some commonsense aspects of the world and have been asking which story of reality—which worldview—best explains them. So far I have suggested three of those features.

First, something is terribly wrong with the world. Things are not the way they are supposed to be, a fact so obvious to everyone it constitutes the nonbeliever's main objection to the existence of God, at least the kind of God Christians believe in.

Second, there is a certain beauty about human beings that sets them apart from everything else—an innate, built-in worth that makes people valuable in themselves and is the source of their unique human rights and their moral obligations toward each other.

Third, even though man is beautiful, he is also broken. He has dignity, even nobility, but he is also cruel. This truth is also obvious. Simply consider the string of excuses and host of strategies we seize upon to dodge our moral responsibility for the bad things we have done. What exactly is it we are trying so hard to explain away? The harder we work to dismiss our fault, the larger it looms. The gnawing sense of guilt remains. We are broken—not like machines that need to be fixed, but like transgressors who need to be forgiven—and we know it.

I have also been saying that only the Christian Story of reality explains these facts adequately. And even though there have been objections raised about this Story (specifically, the problem of evil and the narrowness of Christianity), I have suggested that these are not problems for the Story at all, but make perfect sense once you understand the larger picture, once you see how the world went bad in the beginning. I have also said that the reason the world is not the way it is supposed to be, is that something about man is no longer the way it is supposed to be. Now I would like to tell you precisely how man got broken and how the world went wrong.

The Story tells of a garden and a tree and a snake. This part of the account seems fanciful to many—idyllic orchards, forbidden fruit, talking snakes— and therefore difficult to take seriously. Remember, though, that many things at home in our story simply would not make sense in a story of a different sort. It is not intellectually fair to disqualify the details of one worldview (where God and nonmaterial things are real, and where super- natural things happen) based on standards that would only be appropriate in a very different kind of universe (where only matter is real). One must take the specifics on their own terms in light of their own world. If the real world truly is the kind of world the Story describes, then these particulars do not present a problem in themselves.

Also, let us not get distracted by fine points that may be important to theological specialists whose valuable task is to parse out those particulars, but unnecessarily complicate things for ordinary people trying to get a sense of the big picture. To add a twist to one of Jesus' sayings, we may end up straining at gnats while missing the camel. Theologians may spar about those things, but the larger point is this: There was a real place in a real time when a real rebellion broke out on earth, and that rebellion changed the world and everything in it.

God gave the first man, Adam, a home perfectly suited to his natural needs. He gave him a friend, Eve, to be his proper companion, an able helpmate by his side to share his life with. He gave them rule over the land and its beasts and gave them a meaningful task: to be fruitful, multiply, and subdue. Bring productive order to the earth that had been delivered into their care. With all of that, God gave them something else that was more important than the whole world now at their feet. God gave them himself in friendship.

And here I must pause and express a frustration. I am trying to help you see something that is hard for any of us to imagine because it is so foreign to the way life is for us at the present. I am trying to help us picture what a "just right" world might be like. I do not mean the kind of perfect world children and immature adults imagine, filled with toys and confections with no inconvenient tasks like chores or schoolwork getting in the way of play. Real grownups know a world like that only brings bellyaches and boredom.

I mean the kind of perfect world our hearts have always longed for, even when we cannot quite get it into focus. The longing itself is a clue for us—an ache in our hearts reminding us of the way things used to be, a sign that we were made for something better—though, for the moment, we have lost our way—and a hunger for the world to be that way again. The Story says God has put eternity in our hearts,[1] and that sweet pain may be evidence of it, a primal memory deep in our souls reminding us of the way the world started—good, wonderful, whole, complete.

The world God entrusted to man to rule responsibly over was that way. It was just right. There was no conflict, no toil, no tears, no anguish, no suffering, no dissatisfaction. There were no barriers between Adam and Eve, and there were no barriers between them and their King. The friendship they shared together was perfect. Here is the way the Story describes the unspoiled companionship they felt between each other and with God, "And they were naked, but not ashamed."

All was just the way it was supposed to be, but not immutably so. Things could change. And they did.

There was a prohibition, a single restriction placed on his subjects by the Sovereign, a lone demand made of his children by the Father, a solitary boundary defining the friendship. They could eat the fruit of every tree in the garden but one. It was a reasonable requirement, a minimal mandate. There was no reason to question it, and no natural inducement to disobey it.

Yet there is another player in the Story—an intruder, a deceiver, a tempter, a mortal enemy of the King—who speaks a Terrible Lie.[2] He tells Adam and Eve that the King cannot be trusted. He says the love of God is not genuine and his word is not true. "Don't listen to him," the liar whispers. "Find your own way. Make your own rules. Satisfy your own desires. Freedom awaits you. Be like God."

Man hesitates. He toys with the temptation. He considers the lie. Then he gives in to the deception, first Eve, then Adam. Those wondering exactly what kind of tree it was, or whether "eating the forbidden fruit" was a kind of shorthand for sexual sin or something of that sort, are missing the point. The issue is not that man simply fails to keep the rules. That might matter in sports or in board games, but it is not the measure in relationships. This is a test of trust. It is a test of fealty to a Sovereign, a test of love for a father, a test of faithfulness to a friend.

This one decision—this single act of disobedience, this solitary act of sedition, this lone betrayal—changes everything. Adam and Eve, enticed by the promise of personal autonomy—the allure of the sovereign self— turn against their Lord. The Kingdom is torn by revolt. Rebellion does not bring freedom, though. Instead, it brings brokenness, disgrace, guilt, slavery, and struggle.

Adam and Eve struggle against each other, their harmony shattered, each shifting blame, man to woman, woman to tempter. Man struggles with the ground he was meant to govern that now seeks to govern him. Work becomes toil as the earth fights back with briars and thorns. Woman struggles to bear children in labor and pain, and clashes with the man who now rules her. And in the end—after a lifetime of anguish, suffering, trials, and tears—all will lose the battle when each breathes his last and man's physical form turns to dust. Then he is broken yet again when his soul is torn from his body in death, his self violently split in two.[3]

But there is more than one kind of dying. Adam and Eve are also dead toward God, cut off from the spiritual life that only friendship with God can give. Encounter with the King, once peaceful joy, is now painful shame. No longer fit for Paradise, the traitors are expelled from the garden and banished from his presence.

Death spreads like plague through all mankind. Brother slays brother in cold blood and calm arrogance. Men, proud of their violence, boast of their killings. With each generation, man's rebellion becomes more dramatic. The darkness spreads. One thoughtless act of sin and self-will has changed the world forever.

And now, two objections. The first concerns the tempter, the being behind the voice of the talking snake. "Are you saying," (you might ask) "that there really is a devil who toys with human passion and who teases us into doing evil? That is a bit much."

That is precisely what I am saying. And he does a great deal more than toy and tease. Whether it is "a bit much" or not depends entirely on the kind of world we actually live in. Jesus certainly believed the devil and his vile minions were real, and he encountered—and defeated—them frequently. And if you do not take this part of the drama seriously, then the Story simply will not hold together since, at the heart of things, this is a Story about a worldwide war, and the devil commands the opposing army. The Story makes it quite clear that man's conflict in the visible realm is tied to a battle going on in a realm that is not visible, but is still completely real. And in a literal sense, the things we do not see matter a lot more in this struggle than the things that we do see.[4]

As it turns out, there actually is a Dark Lord—and there are trolls under the bridge, and creatures in the closet, and monsters under the bed. Our primal fears are well founded. There is an evil master, and he commands legions. He is no cartoon character with hoofs and horns and tights and pitchfork. He is pure, unadulterated evil personified.

Satan is real—a powerful spiritual being, the third player in the Story along with God and man. He has invaded God's Kingdom of light to bring his own kingdom of darkness. He gains ground by craftiness and secrecy, and he destroys by lies, accusation, enticement, and subterfuge. If you doubt him, beware. Stealth is his weapon. Satan happily stays in the shadows where he can do his dark business undetected. Underestimate him—or worse, ignore him—to your peril.

Here is the second objection. "What has all this to do with me? I wasn't in that garden. I didn't eat that fruit. Why should I suffer for what someone else did?" But in a certain, very real sense, you were in the garden and you did eat the fruit. We all were and we all did.

And here we come to an important detail that is difficult for moderns (especially Westerners) to grasp, but one that made perfect sense to the ancients. They understood how nations and communities and families function. Each exists as a group and lives as a unit. They prosper together and they perish together because they are knit together as one.

The Story comes to us from ancient people who in some ways saw reality much more clearly than we do. For us, the individual reigns. But that is not how life works. The ancients knew, as John Donne properly put it, that "no man is an island, entire of itself; every man is a piece of the continent, a part of the main."

This notion of one person standing in for the group is not entirely foreign to us, is it? Even today there are circumstances where a single individual's decision is also the group's decision with all sharing the profit or loss together. Parents act on behalf of families, school principals on behalf of students, presidents on behalf of countries. When Congress makes a treaty, each citizen is bound by its provisions and profits by its benefits. When a leader declares war, the leader speaks for the group, and we all are at war together.

And so it was with our first parents. When Adam sinned, we—the human community—sinned. When Eve rebelled, we—her offspring—rebelled. Our entire race was poisoned by our first parents. And so we all are born to corruption, a flaw passed like a vile gene from soul to soul, parent to child, generation to generation.

Adam and Eve, standing in for all yet to be born, in a single act of disobedience plunge all mankind into war against the King. The Terrible Lie enters the world and now lives in every human heart, poisoning each person, turning them against the God who made them. From this day forward, man is "born to trouble as surely as sparks fly upward."[5]

CHAPTER 14

Evil

AND NOW WE COME TO A THORNY MATTER. Given the mess man has gotten himself into, it seems I am forced to face an awkward dilemma with God, especially if I am intent on advocating a God who is both entirely strong and completely good.

Here is the problem. First, God must be a very weak sovereign if he wanted to keep order in his own Kingdom but could not prevent rebellion, either in the beginning or now. Second, it might be he is not weak at all. Maybe he is perfectly capable of preventing the evil, but is indifferent to the pain, the suffering, and the injustice now rampant on the earth. In that case he would be strong, but he would not be good.[1]

At first glance, this seems like an impossible situation for the Christian Story, so much so that some are tempted to think a good and powerful God simply does not exist. If that is what you are wondering, I want to remind you of something I mentioned toward the beginning of our conversation. I said that getting rid of God because bad things happen, though an understandable impulse, does not solve anything. It neither explains the world's brokenness nor helps us repair it. In fact, atheism cannot even make sense of the notion of a "broken" world to begin with, so the problem of evil turns out to be just as lethal for atheism as it appears to be for theism.[2]

But I think we can do better than simply saying the atheist is in the same deep water as the Christian. In fact, I do not think the Christian is in deep water at all. I think the dilemma is a false one. There is more to the Story than what we have considered so far.

I do not think it true that God is weak, nor do I think it true that God is indifferent. But I also do not think it true that a perfectly good God would never permit any evil. And neither, I wager, would you, if you think about it. What I mean to say is that it might turn out there is no conflict at all between the existence of a good God *and* the existence of evil—even appalling evil—and if that's the case, it improves the situation for the Christian Story considerably.

First, though, I must clear up a confusion. The Story presents God as omnipotent, a Being with unlimited power. Some take this to mean that if God were really God he could rise to any challenge. No task would be too difficult, no test too daunting, no request impossible to fulfill. But that is not what omnipotence means.

Omnipotence does mean possessing all power, true enough (omni-*potence*, after all), but it does not mean meeting any challenge. There are some things power cannot accomplish. It does not take much strength to bend a paperclip into a square or to bend it into a circle. But no amount of might will ever allow you to bend it into a square circle. It cannot be done even when strength is unlimited.

When the Story says God is all powerful, it means God can do anything power is capable of doing. Some things are beyond him, so to speak, and the difficulty has nothing to do with power. Square circles are impossible because they, like married bachelors, are contradictions, and it's no limitation on God that he cannot "make" them. Indeed, tasks that are contradictory are not even tasks at all in any meaningful sense. If we ask, "Can God make a rock so big he can't lift it?" (that is, "Can God defeat himself?"), or "Can God make a married bachelor?"[3] we are talking nonsense.

So, when we say God can do anything, we must be careful. Contradictions simply do not qualify—and in a moment you will see why being clear on this detail is so important to our challenge.

Now back to my earlier point. Here is the crux, the key issue: Is it true that a good God always prevents evil as far as he is able to?[4] At first it seems the answer is obviously yes. But think again. Is it possible there could be a circumstance when someone good allows something bad, even when he could prevent it? Is there a chance that, in some cases at least, God might have a good reason to allow evil? Philosophers call this a "morally sufficient reason," and you're already familiar with the basic concept.

Imagine a commando in World War II who is dropped behind enemy lines posing as a German officer so he can get into a concentration camp and destroy the gas chambers. Imagine next that as he mingles with other officers he sees a soldier preparing to execute a prisoner. This is an evil he could stop by simply shooting the soldier, but at what cost? He might save one person, but his mission is to save many. More lives would be lost in the long run if he prevents an individual death, but does not stop the gas chambers from destroying thousands.

So now we are back to our original question. Might a good person allow something evil, even though he could stop it? Clearly, the answer is yes. Even a good person might allow evil he could have prevented if he had a good reason to do so. He might (as we have seen in our example) allow a lesser evil if doing so would prevent a greater evil.

But there is another kind of circumstance in which a good God might allow evil. Let me offer you a different situation, one that every parent is familiar with. On occasion I take my daughter to the doctor to get her shots. This is a misery my daughter must endure (she does not like shots). The pain she experiences in the moment, however, accomplishes a great good in the long run, even though the trade-off is lost on her at the time. I have been a good father even though I have allowed—or even caused—my daughter to suffer, because a greater good—her long-term health and well-being—are the result.

So, the statement, "A good God always prevents evil as far as he is able to," is simply false, isn't it? Instead, it is more accurate to say that a good God always prevents suffering and evil unless he has a good reason to allow it. Sometimes God might allow an evil because it will prevent a greater evil (like with the commando). Sometimes he might allow evil because it will produce a greater good (like with my daughter's shots).

I am not saying that evil can be good, but rather that there may be good reasons to allow bad things. Allowing some evil for a time, for example, may result in a better world in the long run than a world that never had evil to begin with. That certainly is plausible. Note, by the way, that sometimes the evil a good God might allow could be a very big evil indeed. Even so, it could still be acceptable, at least in principle, if the good that results is greater than the evil that's allowed. If this is sound thinking, then God's goodness would not require him to prevent all evil.

We are making progress with our dilemma. It appears we have discovered some loopholes. For one, it may turn out that doubts some people have about God's power have nothing to do with power after all, but with logical absurdities. Second, it's beginning to look like God is not obligated by his goodness to use his power to prevent all evil in every circumstance, but may have morally sufficient reason to allow it in some cases.

Both of these seem plausible, at least in principle. But now we need to put these theoretical possibilities to work in a practical way. What good reason might God have to allow evil in our own world? Though it is always hazardous trying to read God's mind, I would like to suggest a possibility, one that careful thinkers in the past have found compelling.

I said earlier that God created man to share friendship with him. This is not because God needed a companion. A perfect Being does not need anything to be completely satisfied and entirely happy (plus, we will learn later, in an odd sort of way God already had real friendships even before he created anything at all). The reason God is perfectly happy is because he is completely and thoroughly and perfectly good. His happiness flows from his goodness.

No, God did not create the world because he needed anything. Instead, he created it because he wanted to share his own happiness with others. But what sort of being would be capable of sharing God's friendship and happiness?

Think, for a moment, about the kinds of things God has made. Some things he's created—like mountains and rivers and rocks—are inanimate.

They have no life. Other things—like trees and roses and rutabagas—have life, but they have no will. Neither planets nor plants make choices. Instead, their entire existence is governed by physics and chemistry. As mere physical objects, they are pushed and pulled and knocked about by other physical objects in the universe. Since they have no will and make no choices they can have no friendships.

Animals are different, somewhat. They have both life and will, but their ability to choose is of the simplest sort. Because they are conscious we know they have minds, but nothing meaningful follows from their choices because natural impulses govern nearly all of them. Instincts produce bonding, to be sure, but I do not think they produce love or friendship, at least not the kinds that matter in a relationship with God.

Let us call the ability animals have to choose *shallow freedom* because they can't make the kind of choices that matter much. They are neither rational creatures nor moral creatures. They cannot be good, so they cannot be happy in the way God is happy. Since their conduct is driven by natural impulse, not by choosing between true or false or between right and wrong, they cannot make the kinds of decisions that count in friendships. Yes, you could have a sort of friendship with your pet terrier, but it is nothing like the friendships you can have with spouses, children, or closest confidants (though at times you may prefer the company of the terrier).

So, in the beginning the world was filled with wonderful things that would never be able to share in God's happiness. So God made man. Humans are finite, like animals, but personal, like God. Man's choices are not caused by physics or chemistry or instinct. They are his own. They are the product of genuine liberty. Man has what might be called *deep freedom*. He is free to make choices that are not trivial because reasons matter to him. Man is also a moral creature—capable of sharing the kind of goodness that is the basis for God's happiness.

Now let us go a step further. It is hard to be completely certain about things like this, but I have a suspicion that only a creature with deep freedom (one who makes decisions for reasons that are his own) and who is also a moral being (can experience goodness) can have a meaningful friendship with God. In order to share God's happiness, man would have to be able to share his goodness. So God created man morally innocent, without sin, intending man to use his deep freedom to choose obedience, growing in goodness and virtue, becoming more like God himself—both in holiness and happiness. If friendship with God and sharing in his happiness are good things (and it seems they are), then making a creature who could enjoy these things is also a good thing, even if it comes with a liability. And there is the rub.

I think you can see where I am going with this. Our concern has been that since there is evil in the world, either God is not powerful or he is not good. Now it appears that something entirely different may be going on. A solution is beginning to take shape.

When it comes to the problem of evil, there has been a trade-off. Precisely because God is good, he wanted to share his happiness with others. So he created humans with the kind of freedom and the kind of nature that would allow them to grow in goodness, deepening their happiness and their friendship with God. Since happiness depends on goodness,[5] man had freedom to choose the good, but this same freedom also allowed him to choose the bad. This is called *moral freedom*.[6] Put simply, something good made something bad possible (though not inevitable).

It looks now like the tables have turned. Precisely because God is good he made a creature that could go bad. And there is no other way around it. No freedom, no growth in goodness. No growth in goodness, no growth in happiness. So God's own goodness is no longer on the chopping block.[7]

Neither, as it turns out, is his power. Since moral freedom *just is* the possibility of doing good *and* evil, removing the possibility would remove the freedom. It would be impossible for God to create man with genuine moral liberty without any possibility that man would use it for ill. It would be like trying to square the circle—a logically impossible challenge and, therefore, no meaningful challenge at all.

The concern about evil has not been fully resolved, of course. There are unanswered questions, so it is still a problem for the moment, but not the way most people think it is. It turns out there is no necessary contradiction with God's goodness, his power, and the existence of evil, at least not in the Christian Story.

Here is a problem that remains. God's goodness made possible a world that could have badness. As odd as that sounds, we learned a moment ago that this would make sense if God had a good reason to do so. We discovered that one good reason God might allow evil is so he can accomplish a greater good, that maybe a world with some evil would end up being better, in the long run, than one with no evil. I think most people would be willing to admit that human freedom—along with the happiness it can bring—is a great good, even with its liabilities. But is it good enough? Is it a good enough reason to allow all the world's evil in the first place?[8] Was it worth the risk?

That is a fair question, but it is not one we could ever answer on our own. Yes, it sometimes seems there is such a great surplus of evil and suffering that it's impossible to imagine how any greater good could result. We may look around us and think it was not worth the gamble. But there is only one way we could believe that with any confidence. We would need to know every variable that might tip the scales in one direction or another. We do not. Only God can know that.

Consider this. If someone asked if there was a live elephant in the room, that would be a pretty easy question for you to answer. If he asked if there was a flea in the room, though, that would be more difficult.[9] If one landed on your leg and bit you, then you'd know, of course. But if you never found a single flea even though you looked carefully, that would not mean none was there. There still could be plenty of fleas you simply were not able to find.

The point is this. There are some things we are in a good position to know with confidence (if there is an elephant in the room, for example) and other things that are completely beyond us. The answer to the "Was it worth it?" question is like that. And knowing all the reasons God might have to allow evil is a lot more difficult than finding fleas.

Remember I said that when my daughter got her shots, the benefit of the bad-for-good trade-off was lost on her in the moment? I was not merely making a joke. I was offering an insight. It is often hard for us to see how the bad thing God permits in the present could ever bring a greater good in the future. This is because we do not know the future or the infinitely complex set of events that fall like dominoes from our lives into the lives of others. Sometimes decades—maybe even centuries—pass before the balance shifts. This happens often in the Story, since only a God like ours can transform something that starts out evil into something that ends up good.[10]

Because we can never know if freedom was worth the price of evil, this is one of those things we must leave to God. And since we have good reason to believe he exists, and that he is good and wise,[11] I think we are in safe hands with this strategy.

If God had good reason to allow every instance of evil, and if he knew there would be greater good in the world in the long run than if he had not given man freedom to begin with, then it was no gamble at all. That is all we need, I think, to take God off the hook. And that is where the Story leaves it.

Here is what we do know. Man did not use his freedom well. Adam and Eve, capable of living in harmony with God, in friendship under his rule in his Kingdom, betrayed the friendship. Instead of using their freedom to honor God, they used it to rebel.

And now we are at the heart of a central matter in the Story. Parents give children boundaries for reasons. They have insight into how things work that youngsters do not have. They know that if their children disobey, they are likely to break something—maybe just a vase or a picture window, maybe an arm or leg, maybe a valued relationship, maybe an entire life. Disobedience destroys, and sometimes the damage is so great it can never be repaired.

The same is true with God and us. God gives commands for reasons. When we disobey him, we always break something valuable.

Here is the key to understanding the problem of evil: When God's children disobeyed their heavenly Father, they damaged everything. When Adam and Eve rebelled against the King of the universe, they broke the whole world.

This is why there is evil and suffering. Bad things happen in a world that is broken. Every evil that assaults us is the result of rejecting God's rule. It is what the Story calls sin. Sin is the mutation that has twisted and distorted man from his original beauty. Sin is what has broken the world. And a broken world produces broken people and crippled circumstances. Because of sin—man's sin, our sin—the world is no longer the way it is supposed to be.

Note two things, though. First, trouble, hardship, difficulty, pain, suffering, conflict, tragedy, evil—they are all *part* of the Story. It is the reason there is any Story at all. The Story not only explains the evil people do; it predicts it. Our world is exactly the kind of world we'd expect it to be if the Story were true and not just religious wishful thinking.

Second—and more important—*our Story is not over yet.*[12] Evil did not catch God by surprise.

CHAPTER 15

Wrath

IT IS DIFFICULT TO CAPTURE with words the desperate situation man is in.

When Adam and Eve choose rebellion rather than obedience, everything changes. Their likeness to God is sullied, stained, polluted. Their relationship with the Father is ruined, dead. Their relationship with others is warped. Their relationship with creation is compromised. Their souls are morally twisted and broken. And their crimes against their Sovereign incur a debt they cannot pay.

With one act of self-will, man's world turns black. Instead of life, he finds death, his defiance severing his soul's lifeline to God.[1] Instead of freedom, he finds slavery, his corrupted "flesh" now ruling from within and a new master ruling from without, the serpent who man obeyed in the Garden instead of God. Humanity is in the deceiver's grip—held captive by him to do his dark will—and the snake will not let go.[2]

With each generation, man reproduces after his own kind—according to design. All "born of Adam" bear their earthly father's image, now broken. They are rebels, sinners, debtors, slaves. Like sheep, they are prone to wander; like traitors, prone to revolt. In the words of the ancient Hebrew prophet, "All have turned aside, they have together become corrupt. There is no one who does good, not even one."[3] Man, guilty of sedition against his Sovereign, the King of the universe, is utterly lost.

And the King is angry. For man, this is very bad news.

It is hard to imagine anything in religion more repugnant to people than the wrath of God, and it is easy to see why.

The first reason is obvious: God's wrath is unsettling when we are the ones standing in the dock. It is fine when the other guy gets justice, but a very different matter when we get ours. Law-abiding citizens do not object when criminals pay their due. Only the felon finds fault.

Second, we are so well acquainted with our own failures that familiarity has largely removed any deep sense of their gravity. We are inclined to consider ourselves as, generally speaking, basically good folk.[4]

What would happen, though, if we were brought before a judge who had complete knowledge of something as minor as our driving habits? Would we be a bit uneasy? Yet Someone far greater watches—One with perfect knowledge, who executes perfect justice, weighing every person against a perfect Law. Who will be able to say, "I am in the clear. God will find nothing against me"? No, instead he will find mountains—immorality, egotism, rebellion, self-will, deceit, disobedience—amassed from a lifetime of sin.

Here is the last reason we are uncomfortable with the wrath of God. The notion of a "vengeful" God strikes us as inconsistent with a God of love. This seems right at first, but the complaint is based on a misunderstanding. God's love is not a thing in itself, so to speak, but is tied, like all of his attributes, to his goodness, the very goodness we are inclined to question when evil runs rampant. "Why doesn't God do something?" we wonder. Yet we cry foul when we learn God *will* do something decisive about evil and we are the evildoers.

Goodness has different faces. The same virtue that enflames God's love fires his justice. God would not be good if he truly hated evil but was benign toward those who consistently cause it. Justice means exacting an appropriate payment for a crime. No payment, no justice. No justice, no goodness. Is God "vengeful"? No more than any good, fair, noble, just judge who must pass sentence on lawbreakers.

And remember, God's goal with man is friendship. Yet it is difficult to be friends with someone who is constantly, egregiously offending—and doing it on purpose. True, God's wrath is not his most popular quality, but it will do us no good to give it the short-shrift. Too much is at stake.

No, the One who is most holy sees sin most clearly. The One who is perfectly righteous sees the full tragedy of our most "trivial" breaches of goodness. And this is not good news.

Man must pay, but he cannot pay. He must be freed, but slaves cannot free themselves. He desperately needs a rescuer. He needs to be saved by someone who does not himself owe, and who is not himself enslaved.

The Story could have ended here, since God owes no man a pardon. But this is not the end of the Story. It is the beginning. In the dark, there is a ray of light, a veiled promise. Satan has inflicted damage, but the woman's seed will strike the fatal blow.[5] With man lost and helpless and the world terribly broken, God himself steps into the picture to initiate a rescue operation.

PART THREE

JESUS

CHAPTER 16

History

BEFORE WE CAN CONSIDER anything important about the life of Jesus, I must first address a concern that, unless it is put to rest, will make it impossible for us to take seriously anything the Story says about Christ. Our concern is this claim: The Jesus of the Gospels was never a man of history at all, or at least not a man who was anything like the one depicted in the Story.

If this were true, of course, it would be a fatal blow to Christianity. Since imaginary saviors cannot save real people (and that is the point of the Story, after all), then we must take this challenge seriously. That is, we must take the *challenge* seriously (it must be met). However, I do not take the *claim* seriously because the actual facts do not go in that direction at all.

Take, for example, one version of this view that has been especially popular in recent years. I call it the "recycled redeemer" theory. According to this claim, the record we have of Jesus' life is nothing more than a kind of "folklore plagiarism," a mere rehashing of the fictions of ancient mythology.[1] Bits and pieces from the lives of pagan mystery-religion figures—like Mithras, Dionysus, Osiris, Attis, Horus, Adonis—have been recycled and cobbled together (they say) to fabricate the story of the dying and rising god-man from Nazareth.

I think this particular notion is complete nonsense, and I say so not to be dismissive but because the claim is clearly false on a number of counts, and if you look closely at the particulars you will discover this easily. Put simply, the view will not hold up in the face of the facts, since there is hardly a shred of evidence to support it. Indeed, one refutation is so obvious you can work it out on your own simply by reflecting thoughtfully on the claim without ever leaving your easy chair.

First, let me tell you how credentialed historians answer questions like this one and then I will tell you what their academic research has revealed.

Instead of sifting through claims from popular sources that seem to cite each other in endless circles, trained historians go back to the earliest records of these ancient accounts (what they call the "primary sources") to get at the original rendering of the myths themselves. This way they can be clear on exactly what those sources say about Mithras, Dionysus, Osiris, and others. Here is what historians have discovered, in sum.[2]

A close look at the primary sources shows two things that are startling given the popularity of this view. First, the myths that actually *pre-date* Jesus' time bear virtually no resemblance to the particular details of Jesus' life. A host of alleged similarities turn out to be nonexistent. Whatever parallels remain are usually far too general to be significant.

According to historian Tryggve Mettinger, the scholar who has done the most recent exhaustive study of this question, there simply is "no *prima facie* evidence that the death and resurrection of Jesus is a mythological construct, drawing on the myths and rites of the dying and rising gods of the surrounding world."[3]

Second, mythical accounts of the mystery-religion gods that actually do bear some resemblance to Jesus' life unfortunately (for the theory) show up *after* his time. This fact creates a problem for the recycled redeemer view since it looks very much like those stories were copied from the Gospels, not the other way around. Clearly, the child cannot come before the parent. The "recycled" version must appear in the historical record *after* the one it allegedly came from, not *before* it.

Finally—and decisively, it seems to me—there is a logical problem with the recycled redeemer view. This is the one you can work out from your easy chair simply by reflecting on the claim. Let me introduce the point by telling you a remarkable true story about a breathtaking coincidence that is almost too bizarre to believe, yet it really happened.

In 1898, a man named Morgan Robertson published a novel titled *Futility*.[4] The story was a fictional account about a transatlantic voyage of a cruise ship traveling between England and New York. The ship was massive, the largest vessel afloat, and it was considered indestructible. Even so, in the middle of the night in April, with three massive propellers driving the ship forward, the "unsinkable" ship collided with an iceberg and sank to the bottom of the ocean. Because the number of lifeboats on the ship was half of what was needed for its capacity, more than half of its passengers perished. The ship was called the *Titan*.

That is the fiction. Here is the fact. Fourteen years after Robertson published *Futility*, the world's largest luxury liner—the "indestructible" *Titanic*—departed from England on a transatlantic voyage to New York in April. In the middle of the night, the *Titanic*'s triple screws drove the ship into an iceberg, and it sank to the bottom of the ocean. Since the *Titanic* was fitted with less than half the number of lifeboats needed for its capacity, more than half of its passengers were lost.

This real-life coincidence teaches us a crucial lesson that I do not want you to miss. Regardless of the similarities between two accounts of different events, the second cannot simply be dismissed as fabrication merely because the first was a fiction. Whether or not the details of the *Titanic*'s disaster are accurate can only be determined by its own evidence. You may speculate all you like about similarities with the ill-fated fictional *Titan* fourteen years earlier, but that will get you nowhere since it tells you nothing about the reliability of newspaper reports describing the *Titanic*'s demise on April 15, 1912.

Now let's look at this same point from a different direction. Imagine introducing yourself to a stranger and sharing bits of autobiography with him only to have him label you a liar and an imposter. His reason? In the past three months, twelve others tried to pawn off precisely the same story on him. When you offer your driver's license to verify your identity, he ignores it. He has already marked you as a fraud like the rest, no matter what *bona fides* you might produce to change his mind.

In addition to being offended, I suspect you would be a bit mystified. Clearly, the stranger cannot prove you are lying about your identity simply by citing others who lied about theirs. No imposter of the past could logically foreclose on the possibility that you might be the genuine article. That must be decided on separate grounds. To paraphrase C. S. Lewis, one must show *that* a story is false before it makes any sense to speculate on *how* the falsehood originated in the first place.[5]

In the same way, one must first show *that* the historical record of Jesus' life is a fiction before he starts explaining *where* the fiction came from to begin with. That is the logical blunder. Even if someone produced a thousand parallels with Jesus from ancient myths, that alone would not be enough to prove he was just another legend. If the similarities were remarkable, it might raise eyebrows ("Not another one") and invite a closer look. I hope it is clear, though, that it would do nothing on its own to disqualify the historical Christ.

First things must always come first. It will do no good to simply assume Jesus is a myth and then speculate on the origin of the error, but that is precisely what these critics have done. The ancient historical documents about Jesus—principally Matthew, Mark, Luke, and John (there are others[6])—must be assessed on their own merits first, not dismissed with fanciful comparisons to ancient myths of dying and rising gods.

And here is another armchair reflection that might have occurred to you. If you were a first-century fabricator seeking to convince fiercely monotheistic, Torah-observant Jews that their Messiah had arrived, would you draw from pagan accounts of dying and rising gods to make your point, especially when those same Jews expected a king who would conquer, not a Messiah who would be murdered, much less rise from the dead? I think this is unlikely in the extreme.

Put simply, regarding the recycled-redeemer hypothesis, first, the skeptics' facts are unreliable, and second, their thinking is unsound, so their challenge is doubly dead.

It is time to hear from the real historians. What is the verdict about Jesus the man of history from those who are actually skilled and certified in the craft of history? Professional historians do not believe the New Testament account is merely a retelling of ancient myth. Not every historian endorses every detail of the Gospel records, to be sure. Many academics reject the supernatural elements for reasons completely unrelated to the general reliability of the record (that is another issue). However, scholars both liberal and conservative overwhelming agree that Jesus of Nazareth was a man of history and the Gospels, on the main, tell his story accurately.

Note, for one, Will Durant, the Pulitzer Prize-winning historian who wrote the most successful work of history in history, the eleven-volume *The Story of Civilization*. Durant concludes his material on Christ this way:

> No one reading these scenes can doubt the reality of the figure behind them. . . . After two centuries of higher criticism, the outlines of the life, character and teachings of Christ remain reasonably clear and constitute the most fascinating feature in the history of Western man.[7]

The recycled-redeemer crowd asks why we should consider the stories of Mithras, Horus, Attis, and other pagan mystery saviors as fables, yet treat as factual (what they think is) a similar story told of a Jewish carpenter. The answer is simple: There is no good historical evidence for any of the ancient mythological characters and their deeds, but there is an abundance of reliable historical evidence for Jesus. And if the primary source documentation for the man from Nazareth is compelling, then it does not matter how many ancient myths share similarities.

Show me any other person who appears in the historical record with such regularity who turned out, in the final analysis, to be a fiction. Almost no one got his "fifteen minutes of fame" in the ancient world. Why so many mentions regarding Jesus from such a wide variety of sources (Pliny, Tacitus, Lucian, Josephus, to name a few)? Here is why. Jesus of Nazareth was a man *of* history, who made a profound impact *on* history.

So, as it turns out, there is no good reason for any doubt that Jesus was a true man of history or to think the real Jesus was completely different from the one depicted in the Story. According to their own testimony, the Gospel writers were not telling tales, but were reporting their personal encounters[8] with Jesus: "What was from the beginning, what we have heard, what we have seen with our eyes, what we have looked at and touched with our hands concerning the Word of Life [Jesus] . . . what we have seen and heard we proclaim to you also . . . ." The writers were not testifying to myths, but to "sober truth" about events that had "not been done in a corner."[9]

People who think Jesus never existed are simply not acquainted with the ample research done even by secular historians that provide abundant evidence for his life. The idea that Jesus did not exist at all is drivel, and real historians know it.

CHAPTER 17

The God-Man

THERE ARE TWO IMPORTANT THINGS you need to know about Jesus, and neither have anything to do with his teachings in general. What I mean is this. If you remove these two things, then whatever else Jesus taught that you thought was important turns out to be largely inconsequential by comparison. Those who have been taken merely with Jesus' instruction on morality or social justice, for example, have missed the point.[1]

Those two indispensable things are who Jesus was, and what Jesus came to do. They are what theologians call "the person and the work of Christ."

So now the first question: Who was Jesus?

To begin with, Jesus was a true human being. This detail is easy to pass over simply because it is so obvious, but there is a point here. The world was entrusted to man, but the deceiver took it away and now rules instead. A man must war to win it back again. A foul master has made men into slaves. A free man must fight him to set them free. And so, as foretold, the Seed of woman—a genuine human being like ourselves—must do battle with the Snake.[2]

Jesus' humanity is also easy to glamorize, especially in film, but reality is a different matter. Though conceived by a miracle, Jesus still entered the world through labor and blood and pain, like all children. He grew as we all do—through joy and sadness, compassion and anger, rest and weariness, delight and suffering, friendship and betrayal.

All that is true of our essential humanity, and all that we experience—all that we desire, all that we dream; all that discourages us, all that delights us, all that disappoints us; all our hungers and hopes and distresses—all are true of Jesus. He is like us. He is one of us.[3]

So, Jesus is a man. That is the first thing. But there is something more. From the beginning Jesus says things no man is allowed to say, at least not a Jew speaking to other Jews. He says he existed before he was born. He says any sin he pardons is forgiven, as if he is the one any sin has wronged. He says honor due the Father is due him. He says final judgment in the final day falls to him. He says he is drink for the thirsty and bread for the hungry, so they will never thirst or hunger again. He says those who trust in him will live, even if they die.[4]

And here we must attempt something difficult. We must try to imagine we are not modern people but ancient Hebrews. This is important because in our age people are quite comfortable with others saying they are divine in some sense. We may not take them seriously, but nowadays the comment rarely raises an eyebrow. In Jesus' time and place, though, things were different. God was God and man was man. God, eternal; man, temporal. God, infinite; man, finite. God, spirit; man, flesh. God *in* man? God *in* flesh? Well, this was just unthinkable to Jews, and it was unpardonable—a blasphemy deserving death.

If you or I said the kinds of things Jesus said, the words would sound preposterous of course—insane talk, irrational babble. But they do not sound preposterous coming from him, because Jesus does not just talk. He acts. He says he is bread of life, then he multiplies bread to feed thousands. Twice. He says he is resurrection and life, then he raises a dead man to life. He says he is light for the world, then he gives light to the sight of a man born blind.

And here is something else we must not miss. These claims are not about what Jesus' teaching would accomplish. He does not draw attention to his lessons. He draws all attention to himself. These are claims about who Jesus is. "Follow *Me* and live forever." "Believe in *Me* and rise on the last day." "Trust in *Me* and never die."[5]

Jesus is tender and meek, but his claims are not. They are hard and brash and daring and divisive. "Unless you believe that I am He, you will die in your sins." "Before Abraham was born, I am." "He who sees Me sees the One who sent Me." "He who believes in the Son is not judged; he who does not believe has been judged already."[6]

Who is this Jesus, author of such boasts? Everything hinges on the answer to this question. It is the question Jesus asks his own disciples: "Who do you say that I am?" "You are the Christ," Peter answers, "the Son of the living God." And this is Jesus' own answer to that same question at his trial. It earns him a death sentence.[7] You see, *Jesus was not crucified for what he did. He was crucified for who he said he was.*

And now we begin to see why the "Who is Jesus?" question is so important. If Jesus is not who he claimed to be, ignore him as a mad man or (if he knew his claims were false) an imbecile, since he played his charade right to its gruesome end. If his claim is true, however, that changes everything. *"Aut Deus, aut malus homo,"* the ancients wrote. "Either God or a bad man." There is no middle ground.

Yet Jesus was not a bad man. He was not stupid. He was not insane. Those who listened did not laugh. Soldiers sent to arrest him returned empty-handed saying, "No one ever spoke the way this man does."[8] Disciples—saved from a storm that Jesus stilled with a word—were terrified. "Who is this who even the wind and the waves obey?"[9]

"Who is this?" Indeed. This is our question. And the Story gives us our answer. Recall how our Story began: "In the beginning, God created the heavens and the earth." Jesus' story begins this way: "In the beginning was the Word, and the Word was with God, and the Word was God. . . . All things came into being through him, and apart from him nothing came into being that has come into being."[10]

You may have noticed something many people miss if they do not put these two parts of the Story next to each other. This One called "the Word" is the same One who starts the Story in the beginning. He is the main player, the character the Story is all about. He is the person who owns everything, since he made everything. He is the King, and the Kingdom belongs to him.

Then further down we read, "And the Word became flesh, and dwelt among us, and we beheld His glory, glory as of the only begotten of the Father, full of grace and truth."[11] This, I think, is the greatest line in the Story. Making the world from nothing was a stunning work of wonder, to be sure. God becoming one of us, however, walking with us, being near us—knowing human joy, sharing human sorrow—is beyond wonderful. It is sublime.

The God who began the Story, the God who made everything, is the same God who came down, who became flesh, who entered history as a baby born in Bethlehem.[12] Jesus is a man, but he is also God. He is not *a* God, but *the* God. He is the man who God became.[13] He is the one person who is completely human, yet fully divine.[14]

And here we come face-to-face with the oddest—and therefore, the most awkward—notion in the Story, the idea that even though God is one, inside of him (so to speak) there is more than one conscious self. He is both in heaven and on earth at the same time, as unusual as that sounds. That is not something that could ever be true of us, but that is because we are not God.

It is tempting here to think that part of God stayed in heaven and part of him came to earth, while still another part was both in heaven and on earth. But this would be an entirely incorrect way to talk about God. Since God is not made of pieces, parts of him cannot be here and there. We might offer that the Father *stayed* in heaven while the Son *came* to earth while the Spirit *remained* everywhere, and that would be a bit better, I guess, but still not just right. That is all part of the oddness since, as we've seen, God is unique.

For now we will simply say that there is one God, and he is tri-personal— the Father, the Son, and the Holy Spirit, making up what has come to be called the Trinity. Though the Father and the Son and the Spirit are the same One, their conscious selves are so distinct they can talk with each other, and cooperate with each other, and love each other, the same as you and me.

I think this will serve for the moment as a kind of theological shorthand to cover the bases. The great councils of the church labored with many carefully crafted words to say it just right, and you may consult them for more precision.[15]

It's a good thing God is Triune, strange at it seems to us. You may recall I said earlier that a perfect Being like God does not need anything to be completely satisfied and entirely happy. He did not need us to be friends since, because of the Trinity, he already had real friendships within himself before the world began. And he did not need us in order to love since, because of the Trinity, love was shared between the Divine persons from eternity past.

This is why only Christians can rightly claim, "God *is* love." If love, at its core, is selfless giving, there could be no love without someone for God to give love to. "If God was a single person," Lewis noted, "then before the world was made, he was not love."[16]

Love is not a virtue of solitary selves. It cannot be known alone, but lives only in the sharing. If God is not Triune, he cannot love until he creates. Thus, love would be a quality he gains, not an unchangeable moral perfection deep in his being. This is a problem, by the way, for the Muslim understanding of God. He can *show* love, but he cannot *be* love.

No, God did not *need* us; he wanted to *include* us. He cannot do that, though, unless he solves a problem.

I mentioned that one reason God entered our world was so man could battle the Snake and undo what the deceiver had done. That, in a sense, is an earthly reason. But there is another reason, a heavenly one. Man owed a debt to God, and man must pay. Yet what kind of person could make a boundless payment to cover an endless punishment, a penalty due for the sins of an entire world? A human must pay the price for sin, but only God is able. The gap between man and God must be bridged, and that can only be done by the God-man. As one has said, "For in giving His Son, He was giving Himself."[17] Not a God far off, over there, out of reach, completely "other." God near. God here. Immanuel, God with us. God came down.

Now we come to another wrinkle in our Story. I would like to say just a bit more about what was involved when God "came down." How did this happen? It could only happen if something unimaginable, yet wonderful, took place: God got small.

Think for a moment of how you would speak to a frightened child.

You would crouch down. You would get low. You would stoop to his level to gently calm him and draw him to yourself. It's the natural thing to do.

This is precisely what God has done. To reach out to frightened, lost humanity, God crouched down. He came down. He got low. Listen to the Story:

> Christ Jesus, who, being in very nature God, did not consider equality with God something to be grasped, but made Himself nothing, taking the very nature of a servant, being made in human likeness. And being found in appearance as a man, He humbled Himself and became obedient to death—even death on a cross.[18]

The Story is saying this: Even though the Son never ceased being God, still he surrendered his divine rights. He laid them aside. He let them go. Like a king who—out of love—removed his crown, set aside his scepter, took off his royal robes, donned the garb of a common beggar, and lived among the poorest of his subjects. Never ceasing to be king, he got low, so low he willingly died the death of a despised criminal—all to serve his own.

That is what happened. God got small—an unimaginable sacrifice. If you or I traded perfect paradise for the darkest dungeon it would not begin to approach what God did—stooping down, getting low, humbling himself in human flesh.

Note carefully: This is not the Jesus of Islam. This is not the Jesus of Mormonism. This is not the Jesus of the Jehovah's Witnesses. This is not the Jesus of the New Age. Those are all very different stories.

CHAPTER 18

The Rescue

NOW TO OUR SECOND QUESTION: What did Jesus come to do? Since there is more debate on this than there ought to be, we must first correct a misunderstanding. Sometimes knowing what Jesus did not come to do is almost as important as knowing what he did come to do, because a wrong understanding of the first can lead to confusion on the second.

So let us be clear. Jesus did not come to help us get along or teach us to take care of the poor or to restore "social justice."[1] To some, this assertion is a bold stroke, since they have been told just the opposite. This is because there are many noble people who are drawn to Jesus for his moral excellence (as they should be). However, often their admiration of his civic virtue has distracted them from a more important matter.

Their mistake is thinking that Jesus came principally to teach us how to live a better life. He did not. God had already sent many before with the kind of advice we need to hear, and there was no point in his personally coming down merely to repeat what had already been said. No, Jesus came for a different reason.

What I am going to say next will come as a shock to some, but here it is. You can eliminate every single thing Jesus ever said in his life about the poor and social justice, and still you will not undermine his main message one bit. As severe as that may sound, this is precisely what one of Christ's closest followers actually did.

The Gospel of John is the last biography written on Jesus, and it came to us from his last surviving apostle, the "beloved" disciple John, a member of Jesus' intimate inner circle. Many think it the most elegant summary and most definitive statement of who Jesus was and what he came to do. Yet you can read from John's first sentence to his last and you will not find a single word about helping the poor or restoring social justice. Not one. In John's lone reference to the poor, Jesus is actually somewhat dismissive of them.[2] That is not because he doesn't care about them, but because he is comparing their situation with something far more important.

This observation about John's account in itself seems enough to make the point about Jesus' focus, but let's go a bit further. Jesus gave four major discourses—the Sermon on the Mount, the Bread of Life Discourse, the Olivet Discourse, and the Upper Room Discourse.[3] Only in the first does he mention the poor at all. Yet even here there are two qualifiers you must keep in mind.

First, in his Sermon on the Mount Jesus commends not the poor *per se* but rather the poor *in spirit*. To them, he says, belongs the Kingdom of Heaven. There is a reason the Kingdom belongs to them—not because they are poverty stricken (their income is irrelevant to Jesus), but because they are morally broken and they know it.[4] That is what "poor in spirit" means. Picture the tax collector in Jesus' parable—hardly a destitute man—beating his breast pleading, "God, have mercy on me, a sinner."[5] This man proclaiming his spiritual poverty goes away justified, Jesus says, while the Pharisee, whose spiritual arrogance clouds his genuine spiritual need, does not.

The second qualifier I want you to keep in mind about Jesus' comments on the poor is this: In the vast majority of cases where Jesus mentions the poor, he does so not to commend the poor as such, but to make a point about something else—hypocrisy, a widow's generosity, Zacchaeus's repentance, the rich young ruler's confusion, or a lesson about the afterlife.[6] Even when he mentions them, the plight of the poor simply was not the focus of Jesus' teaching.

Now, we must not conclude from this that Jesus didn't care about the poor and so we need not care either. He cared very much about them, and the Story has much to say about their situation. Do not miss, though, that he also cared about the rich and powerful. Jesus helped *everyone* and *anyone* who came to him—poor beggar or prostitute, wealthy tax collector or Pharisee. The divide for Jesus was not between the poor and the rich, but between the proud and the repentant, regardless of income or social standing. Miss that, and you miss everything.

These are the facts we must face if we are to get Jesus right. "Social justice" is not the Gospel. It was not Jesus' message. It was not why he came. His real message was much more radical. Jesus' teaching—and the Story itself—focuses on something else. Not on the works of *Christians* but rather on the work of *Christ*. That is what the Story teaches.

And so our question remains: Why did God come down? What was the reason he became a man? What did he come to earth to do? The Story tells us.

I want you to think for a moment about what the Story says about Christmas. Now when I say "Christmas," I am not speaking of any of those things that usually come to mind when you think about the birth of Christ. I do not want you to think, for example, about shepherds or wise men or stables or mangers or anything like that. Those things all have their place, but they have nothing at all to do with my point.

I am talking about something in the Story you probably have never noticed. I want you to consider the most important Christmas verse in the Story that you will never see on a Christmas card and you will never hear in a Christmas pageant because it is not in the accounts of Jesus' birth at all. In fact, it does not appear anywhere in the record of his life. Instead, you find it in a dark and foreboding passage that speaks of blood and sacrifice and death. It is a section of the Story recounting a ghastly, grisly system of slaughter where bulls and goats were bled out, their innocent lives forfeit on behalf of others who were the guilty ones.

Now, I think it is obvious to just about everyone that animals can never really pay for people at all. The system of sacrifice God gave to the Hebrews, as important as it was, served only as a kind of sop, a temporary measure to cover man's moral wound for the moment. It would never do in the long run, and it was not meant to. No, man owes the debt, and in the long run man, not creatures, must pay. And only a sinless man—someone with no debt of his own—could cover the debt of another. And only a man who was more than a man could ever pay for the sins of multitudes.

And this brings us to the most important Christmas verse you will never hear on Christmas. Here it is:

Therefore, when Christ came into the world, he said: "Sacrifice and offering you did not desire, but a body you prepared for me; with burnt offerings and sin offerings you were not pleased. Then I said, 'Here I am—it is written about me in the scroll—I have come to do your will, O God.'"[7]

Note the opening words of this passage: "When Christ came into the world . . ." The Story is saying that on that first Christmas, in some incredible way the eternal Son of God in a baby's body said to his Father, "Here I am. I will do as you have asked. I accept the body you have prepared for me, the body that will bleed out in perfect payment for sin."

And this is the answer to our question. This is why Jesus came to earth. God's Son surrendered his sinless human self to be the future unblemished offering to perfectly and completely save sinners.

And this we do find in the birth narratives, everywhere. God tells Joseph that Mary "will give birth to a son, and you will give him the name Jesus, because he will save his people from their sins." In the field that first Christmas night the angel tells the shepherds, "Today in the town of David a Savior has been born to you. He is the Messiah, the Lord." Zacharias prophesies over his son, the infant John Baptist, saying John would prepare the way for "the Lord," and "give his people the knowledge of salvation through the forgiveness of their sins." Thirty years later John points at the Lord Jesus Christ and says, "Behold, the Lamb of God who takes away the sin of the world."[8]

Each of these events echoes our unsung Christmas verse: "A body you prepared for me." The Lord. The Christ. The Savior. Emmanuel. God with us, who would die for us. The Lamb of God.

So, the Story tells us the precise reason the Son came to earth. Not to teach love and peace and care for the poor, but to submit himself to something unspeakably violent and brutal. That is why every crèche ought to have a cross hanging over it, because Jesus was born to die. And on this point Jesus speaks clearly:[9]

- "God did not send his Son into the world to condemn the world, but to save the world through him."
- "The Son of Man came to seek and to save the lost."
- "I have not come to call the righteous, but sinners to repentance."
- "I lay down my life so that I may take it again. No one has taken it away from me, but I lay it down on my own initiative."
- "The Son of Man did not come to be served, but to serve, and to give his life as a ransom for many."

I want you to think carefully about Jesus' last statement, because there are three questions we must answer to understand his meaning. The first is, "What is a ransom?" Well, a ransom is the price paid to purchase a hostage or a slave. A ransom buys a body. Second, "Whose body does Jesus buy with the ransom?" He buys those who are held hostage. He pays a price to purchase sinners, rebels, and slaves. Finally, "What is the price he will pay?" Jesus will buy bodies by surrendering his own body. "A body you prepared for me." He will sacrifice himself to save others.

So, Jesus came to earth to save sinners. The statement is so common to our ears, it is easy to miss its significance. *Save* means to "rescue from imminent danger." Jesus came to rescue us because we were in danger. What was that danger? What was Jesus rescuing us from? Here is the answer. Jesus did not come to rescue us from our ignorance or our poverty or our oppressors or even from ourselves. Jesus came to rescue us from the Father.[10]

Remember, the King is angry. He is the one who is offended. He is the one who is owed. He is the Sovereign we have rebelled against, the Father we have disobeyed, the friend we have betrayed. And that is a dangerous place for us to be. Jesus said, "Do not fear those who kill the body, but are unable to kill the soul, but rather fear him who is able to destroy both soul and body in hell." Later in the Story we learn, "It is a terrifying thing to fall into the hands of the living God."[11]

That is the bad news. And it is very bad news, to be sure. Yet without the bad news, the good news is not good. And the good news is very, very good. Here it is: The Father has mounted a rescue operation. There has been an invasion.[12] God came down. "A body you prepared for me."[13]

Jesus' life was filled with many extraordinary deeds, so many, one of his disciples wrote, the world itself could not contain the books needed to record them.[14] But there are two particular things Jesus did that were vital to the rescue.

First, Jesus lived the life we should live but do not. We rebel; he submitted. We sin; he obeyed. We live for self; he lived for the Father. We falter; he succeeded. He had no hint of sin, no darkness, no shadow. As one has put it, "He remained free, uncontaminated, uncompromised."[15] Jesus never failed, obeying even to the death. This no one has ever done. There was no one like him.

Second, Jesus made a trade. He took his perfect life and he traded it for our rotten lives. He gets our badness—and the judgment and punishment that go with it. We get his goodness. We take his place, and he takes our place.

If that seems hard to imagine (and I understand completely if it does), let me offer something that might help. On a flight from Jacksonville to Miami I spoke with a dear Muslim woman about the differences between the God of Jesus and the God of Mohammed. I said that both were holy and both demanded we be holy too, and there will be justice to pay because we are not. But on this issue of justice, I said, we come to an important distinction.

I asked the Muslim woman to imagine our plane being hijacked and the terrorists trying to drag her out onto the tarmac to kill her in front of cameras for all the world to see. I then asked her to imagine that I put my own body between hers and the attackers and said, "Don't take her. Take me instead." She said she could not imagine anyone doing that for her.

Yet this, I told her, is what God has done in Jesus. To satisfy justice, God came down. Not Allah; Yahweh. Not Mohammed; Jesus. God stepped out of heaven and dwelt among us—"A body you prepared for me"—and said to the Father, "Take me instead." That was the trade.

The trade took place on a small outcropping of rock outside the walls of ancient Jerusalem. It was called Golgotha, the place of the skull. We know it as Calvary, the place of the cross.

CROSS

CHAPTER 19

Footsteps

BEFORE WE SAY ANYTHING about Jesus' death, we must look briefly at some of the steps in his life leading up to it since, as we have seen, what Christ accomplished by how he lived is as important as what he accomplished by how he died. The two are inseparable, and the rescue depends on both—Jesus' death and Jesus' life. Whenever there is a trade, there are always two sides, two things being exchanged, one for the other. What Christ received from us—guilt—brought him death. What we receive from him—goodness—brings us life. The goodness we get comes from the merit Jesus earned, and Jesus' goodness permeated every detail of his life. We have already touched on this point.

But there is another reason to pause and follow Jesus' footsteps in the Story for a bit. Certain sayings of Jesus and certain events of his life are so familiar to so many, it is easy to forget that those sayings and events were embedded within the ebb and flow of a genuine human life. I do not want you to think of Jesus as a mystical drifter appearing out of the fog, spouting spiritual sayings and religious proverbs. We must never forget that in many ways Jesus' life was just like ours. He was a real person who breathed, walked, slept, ate, laughed, and wept. Getting a feel for the flow of that life gives substance and depth to the drama.

The Story tells us that Jesus of Nazareth begins his life in an astonishing way. He is born of a virgin, something that had never happened before, nor since. Jesus is unique. A miraculous birth should not surprise us, though. Something unusual like this is to be expected for such an unusual event— God entering the world. What was not expected, though, was that the One who made the entire universe would enter history quietly, in humble circumstance. Yet when we think about it, that makes perfect sense too. God was, after all, getting small, stepping down, bowing low.

The place of Jesus' birth is a modest village of no consequence, Bethlehem, "little among the clans of Judah."[1] His crib is a livestock feeding trough filled with straw, the same bedding used by the animals resting around him. His parents are the poorest of the poor and his first visitors, shepherds, are of Israel's lowliest vocation.

Though the setting is unremarkable, the occasion is not. The infant is no ordinary child, as each player in the Story makes clear. The information the angel Gabriel gives to Jesus' mother, the message of the heavenly heralds at his birth, the words of Simeon and Anna when Jesus is presented at the temple eight days after he was born, and the remarkable visit from the magi, all resonate with the same message.[2] This infant is God come to earth. He is the promised Redeemer, the Messiah of Israel. He is the rescuer, the Savior of the world.

Even so, Jesus' boyhood is quiet. His "lost years" are not lost at all, just uneventful. Contrary to some fanciful accounts, Jesus works no miracles as a child, but waits until he begins his public ministry, astonishing his neighbors who had watched him grow up an ordinary boy.[3] We know only that he lives under the guidance and protection of his family in Nazareth and grows in wisdom and stature and in favor with God and men.[4] His wisdom, of course, is beyond his years. Even at twelve, he amazes the elders in the temple—his "Father's house"—with his questions, and astonishes them with his answers and his understanding.[5]

When Jesus is about thirty years old, John the Baptist begins preaching in the wilderness along the Jordan, announcing that there is one in Israel's midst who is so much greater than John he is not worthy even to untie his sandal. Soon Jesus takes his place with the lowly and is baptized by John.

He is then taken by the Spirit into the wilderness to face—and defeat—the devil and his deceptive temptations.

When he returns from the wilderness, Jesus begins his work, identified by John as "the Lamb of God who takes away the sin of the world."[6] His popularity accelerates and soon eclipses that of John, the forerunner, who gladly steps aside for Jesus. By the time of his first great discourse, the Sermon on the Mount,[7] Jesus is a phenomenon. Unconventional from the outset, he incites curiosity and amazement wherever he goes. His following grows rapidly, but knowing that the people's loyalties run shallow, Jesus does not entrust himself to any.[8] The masses will eventually become disenchanted.

Delightful for many, Jesus is also divisive. He challenges the practices and the prejudices of the religious establishment and he openly confronts its leaders for their lack of genuine spiritual substance. This endears him to the common people who flock to him in great numbers, but those of influence publicly chastise the "ignorant" crowds and begin their plans to silence Jesus, the troublemaker.[9]

Yet Jesus does not yield to anyone's agenda. He speaks the truth with confidence and authority, investing old teaching with fresh insight. His dramatic miracles of physical healing, casting out demons, controlling the forces of nature—even raising the dead—confirm his personal claims as the anointed Messiah, the Son of God—the Divine come to earth in human flesh.[10]

As time passes, though, the tide of popular opinion turns against Jesus. He does not just criticize the leaders who, unmoved by his miracles, now attribute his power to Satan.[11] He also condemns the crowds as wicked and sinful.[12] He speaks more and more in parables to obscure his meaning from the unrepentant.[13] After miraculously feeding thousands, he delivers what has come to be called the Bread of Life Discourse,[14] claiming to be the living bread that came down out of heaven. Refusing to allow the crowds to forcibly install him as a conquering king,[15] Jesus laments openly that they come to him merely to have their stomachs filled. There is no sense of spiritual poverty, no genuine hunger for the one Bread that fills the heart forever, the food that brings eternal life, Jesus himself. They are only interested in material concerns. His listeners respond with shock, disappointment, and derision. It becomes clear that following Jesus brings hardship and difficulty, not glory, power, and prosperity. The people turn away from him in large numbers and most of his disciples desert him. Though the Twelve remain, Jesus notes that one "is a devil."[16] A time of growing opposition now awaits him.

In the last year of Jesus' life his conflict with the people, especially the religious leadership, intensifies. Jesus leaves nothing untouched, rebuking religious self-righteousness more than anything else. He attacks their conduct, their doctrine, the way they dress, anything that speaks of shallow religious piety that hides true spiritual poverty.[17] He says they are like pristine tombs concealing rotting corpses.[18] Jesus has patience with repentant sinners and those with weak faith, but he has none for religious hypocrisy. Spiritual pride—whether from the rich or the poor—hardens the heart, preventing a humble admission of guilt. It is the most pernicious obstacle to restoring an authentic friendship with the Father. Jesus' unrelenting assault hardens the opposition.

As the group of Jesus' followers dwindles, he withdraws, spending more time in obscure areas and gentile regions while investing himself in training the Twelve. Peter's confession that Jesus is the Messiah, the Son of God, is a testimony to the Apostles' deepening commitment to this mysterious man.[19] He gives them a glimpse of his glory at the Transfiguration,[20] then begins to talk plainly of his death that will come soon, and also of his resurrection. These words, though, make no sense to them. They do not understand what rising from the dead means since they simply cannot conceive that their Messiah could be killed.[21]

The circumstances ripen for disaster, and Jesus' hour rapidly approaches. As Calvary looms before him, Jerusalem is now Jesus' only objective. He knows what awaits him there. The raising of Lazarus intensifies the resolve of his enemies, who now aggressively plot his death.[22] The Triumphal Entry on Palm Sunday creates a surge of attention, but the celebration is short-lived. Before the week is out the crowds demand his death, trading "Hosanna" for "Crucify him." In spite of the imminent danger to his life,

Jesus continues to stand boldly and publicly against religious hypocrisy and its root cause, unbelief.

In a matter of days the Messiah will be dead. Jesus spends some of the time with the ones he loves the most, those to whom he has given virtually every waking moment for over three years. He gathers them close for a last Passover meal and for final prayer, preparing them each—including himself—for the dark day ahead. Jesus' life will soon be in the hands of those who hate him, but those hours tick by slowly.

And here we must be clear. It is the Father, not Jesus' enemies, who is in control, and Jesus knows this. He is not a victim. No one takes his life from him. Not the Jews. Not the Romans. He gives it willingly and purposefully.[23] It is his choice. It is what he wants. It is the reason he was born.

Passion week is not only the end of Jesus' journey, it is the final resolution of thousands of years of prophecy, promise, and expectation as the last act of the drama of Jesus' life begins to play out. From the very beginning, as predicted by the ancient Hebrew prophets, a divine plan has been unfolding. Soon a transaction will take place, planned since before the Story began, before even the dawn of time. For Jesus, though, this means betrayal, humiliation, acute physical suffering, and unimaginable emotional agony.

CHAPTER 20

The Trade

NOW I WANT TO ATTEMPT something difficult. I want to explain how a somewhat ordinary execution (and I say "ordinary" only because crucifixions happened frequently in Jesus' time) turned out to be one of the most significant events of all time.

First the ordinary part. Crucifixion is a cruel form of execution. It is generally reserved for slaves and rebels. The victim is often brutally flogged, then stripped naked and fastened to the beams with square, wrought-iron nails. They are driven through the front of each wrist into the *patibulum* crossbeam, severing the median nerve, causing searing pain.[1] The feet are stacked one upon the other against the vertical *staticulum*, and a spike is hammered through both arches. There the criminal hangs, exposed to the elements and to the scorn and ridicule hurled at him by soldiers and mocking bystanders.

Death is agonizing and slow, the result of shock, exposure, and, eventually asphyxiation. To ease the pain in the feet, the victim hangs from the nails in his wrists. But hanging from the cross constricts the diaphragm, hindering breathing. The only way to exhale and get another breath is to pull against the nails in the wrists and push down with the legs, driving the victim's full weight against the spikes piercing his arches, and causing his scourged flesh, hanging in ribbons from his back, to scrape against the ragged timber. The agonizing effort could go on for days. When exhaustion eventually overtakes the victim, he suffocates. Broken legs mercifully hasten death.

For Jesus, though, there is more. The pain of the cross pales in the face of a greater anguish. There is a deeper torment that cannot be seen, one no movie can capture and no words can adequately express. It is more excruciating than the nails pinning Jesus' body to the timbers, more dreadful than the lashes that ripped his flesh from his frame. It is a dark, terrible, incalculable agony—an infinite misery—as God the Father unleashes his fury upon his sinless Son as if Jesus were guilty of an immeasurable evil.

Why punish the innocent One?

Nailed to the top of the cross is an official notice called a *titulus*. It is a public declaration of Jesus' crime of sedition that is posted at the place of punishment. It says, "This is Jesus of Nazareth, King of the Jews."[2] The cross is punishment for that crime and payment of Jesus' debt to Caesar.

When a debt was owed in the first century, a "certificate" of the debt was made, much like the notice placed above Jesus' head. When the obligation was settled, it was officially resolved with a single Greek word placed upon the parchment's face: *tetelestai*. It meant completed, paid, finished, done. Archaeologists have unearthed ancient receipts that have been "canceled out" in this way using the word *tetelestai* or its abbreviation.[3]

Being King of the Jews is not the real crime Jesus pays for, though. Hidden to all but the Father is another certificate "nailed," so to speak, to that same cross. The Story says it is a record not of Jesus' debt, but a rap sheet, of sorts, "consisting of decrees against *us*," that is, against you and me.[4] It is a record of debts that will be displayed before the world at the very end of the Story, at a great judgment of all the dead[5] who stand before an imposing, white throne and are put on trial. Each of the dead is judged by his own behavior, not by comparing one person with another but simply by a raw accounting of each person's conduct recorded in books open for all to see. Every misdeed has been logged, every sin has been written down, and every careless word has been noted.[6]

There is a reason for this dark event at the close of history. As we have seen, if God is good, he *must* punish the guilty, and if he is good he can punish *only* the guilty. It should be clear, then, that God's goodness is good news for the innocent but is not good news for the lawbreakers, the unrighteous, and the sinners. Now, that may be comforting to those who count on faring well in the final assessment, but that is only because they do not quite realize how their lives will actually look when the light shines brightly into every corner, and every act, motive, and desire is laid bare before God and the world.[7] Glance quickly around a dimly lit room and all may seem in order. Shine a bright beam into the corners, though, or under the sofa, and you will see a different sight.

In the same way, none will find safe harbor in his own merit since all things hidden will be revealed, and the Story is quite clear on this point. In the final reckoning, every man will be shown to be a debtor to God—something each of us already knows deep in our own hearts.

Before that white throne, each person who is judged by his own behavior is found guilty,[8] the record in the books silencing every appeal. It will be clear to all that God is justified when he speaks and blameless when he judges.[9] The books leave no room for debate, no ground for petition or plea. No one escapes the guilty verdict save those whose names are written in another book that is also opened, the Book of Life. Those listed there are as guilty as the rest, to be sure, but their debt is not held to their account. It has already been paid. Their rap sheets, their lists of decrees against them, have been nailed to Jesus' cross, their ponderous chronicle of offenses pinned upon Christ himself. Jesus told us to pray, "Father, forgive us our debts . . ." This is how God is able to do that.

In the darkness that shrouds Calvary from the sixth to the ninth hour, a divine transaction is taking place. Jesus makes a trade with the Father. Punishment adequate for all the crimes of all of humanity—every murder, every theft, every lustful glance, every hidden act of vice, every modest moment of pride, every monstrous deed of evil—punishment adequate for every crime of every man or woman who ever lived, Jesus takes upon himself as if he is guilty of all.

In the end, the cross does not prevail. Arguably, Jesus does not die of exposure, or loss of blood, or asphyxiation. Rather, when the full payment is made, when the last of the debt of those who trust in him melts away, when the justice of God is fully satisfied, Jesus simply dismisses his spirit into the Father's hands and dies.[10] But before he does, a single word falls from his lips. It is the word *tetelestai*.

Jesus' solitary word requires three English words to translate: "It is finished."[11] Do not misunderstand, however. Jesus is not collapsing in exhausted relief at the end of suffering. The ordeal is done, true enough, but the Son of God rejoices not in what is *over*. He celebrates, rather, what has been *accomplished*. His words, precisely rendered, mean, "It has been and will forever remain finished."[12] Christ's torment has not simply ended. His goal has been reached; his task has been achieved. The divine transaction is complete. Jesus takes our guilt. We take his goodness. That is the trade. And its effect extends forward, continues on, and changes the world forever.

Theologians use different words to describe different aspects of what took place in Christ's single act of submission and sacrifice that cost him his life. They use terms like justification or substitution or redemption or propitiation, and each is rich with meaning of its own, and that richness is worthy of exploring and pondering. For now, though, we will simply call it what Christians of the past have called it, the "Marvelous Exchange."

The Story puts it this way, "God made him who had no sin to be sin for us, so that in him we might become the righteousness of God,"[13] and, "For Christ also died for sins once for all, the just for the unjust, so that he might bring us to God,"[14] and, "In him we have redemption through his blood, the forgiveness of sins, in accordance with the riches of God's grace,"[15] and many other statements such as these.

Let me offer another way of making this same point.[16] Imagine, for a moment, a king who, having discovered a theft in the royal treasury, decrees that the criminal be publicly flogged as payment for the crime. When soldiers haul the thief before the king as he sits in his judgment seat, there in chains crouches the frail form of the king's own mother.

Without flinching, he orders the old woman to be bound to the whipping post in front of him. When she is secured, he stands up, lays down his imperial scepter, sets aside his jeweled crown, removes his royal robe, then steps down and enfolds the tiny old woman with his own body. Bearing his back to the whip, he orders the punishment to commence. Every blow meant for the criminal lands with full force upon the bare back of the king until the last lash falls.

In like manner, in those dark hours when Christ hung from the cross, the Father took those who would put their trust in Jesus and wrapped them in his Son who shielded them, taking every blow that they deserve. You see, there are actually three passions woven together in this single act of Divine surrender. The passionate intensity of God's anger at us for our sin collides with the passionate intensity of God's love for us, causing the passionate intensity of the agony of the cross to be shouldered by God himself in human form.

This was not an accident. It was planned. The prophet Isaiah described it seven hundred years earlier:[17]

> *Surely he took up our pain*
> *and bore our suffering,*
> *yet we considered him punished by God,*
> *stricken by him, and afflicted.*
> *But he was pierced for our transgressions,*
> *he was crushed for our iniquities;*
> *the punishment that brought us peace was upon him,*
> *and by his wounds we are healed.*
> *We all, like sheep, have gone astray,*
> *each of us has turned to our own way;*
> *and the* LORD *has laid on him*
> *the iniquity of us all.*

Countless others have put it well in their own words since then. Few have done so as poignantly as Augustus Toplady in this hymn:[18]

> *From whence this fear and unbelief?*
> *Hath not the Father put to grief*
> *His spotless Son for me?*
> *And will the righteous Judge of men*

Condemn me for that debt of sin
Which, Lord, was charged on Thee?

Complete atonement Thou hast made,
And to the utmost Thou hast paid
Whate'er Thy people owed;
How then can wrath on me take place,
If sheltered in Thy righteousness,
And sprinkled with Thy blood?

If thou hast my discharge procured,
And freely in my room endured
The whole of wrath divine;
Payment God cannot twice demand,
First at my bleeding Surety's hand,
And then again at mine.

Turn then, my soul, unto thy rest!
The merits of thy great High Priest
Have bought thy liberty;
Trust in His efficacious blood,
Nor fear thy banishment from God,
Since Jesus died for thee.

And here, I hope, something important is beginning to come into focus. The idea that there can be only one way to rescue man from his terrible trouble is beginning to look more reasonable after all. This singular, unique, miraculous, historical event on Calvary explains what has understandably troubled many, causing them to think poorly of the message Christians have always called "good news." *The trade explains why Jesus is the only way of salvation.*

Most ailments need particular antidotes. Increasing the air pressure in your tires will not fix a troubled carburetor. Aspirin will not dissolve a tumor. Cutting up credit cards will not wipe out debt that is already owed. If your water pipes are leaking, you call a plumber, not an oncologist, but a plumber will not cure a cancer. Any adequate solution must solve the problem that needs to be solved, and singular problems need singular solutions. Some antidotes are one-of-a-kind cures for one-of-a-kind ailments. Sometimes only one medicine will do the job, as much as we may like it to be otherwise.

Mankind faces a singular problem. People are broken and the world is broken because our friendship with God has been broken, ruined by human rebellion. Humans, you and I—are guilty, enslaved, lost, dead. All of us. Everyone. Everywhere. The guilt must be punished, the debt must be paid, the slave must be purchased. Promising better conduct in the future will not mend the crimes of the past. No, a rescuer must ransom the slaves, a kindred brother must pay the family debt, a substitute must shoulder the guilt. There is no other way of escape.

This is why Jesus of Nazareth is the only way to God, the only possible source of rescue. *He is the only one who solved the problem.* No other man did this. No other person could. Not Mohammed. Not the Buddha. Not Krishna. Not anyone else. Only Jesus of Nazareth could save the world. Without him, we are crushed under our overwhelming debt. Without him, every single one of us would have to pay for our own crimes, and that would take eternity. Jesus alone, the perfect Son of God, paid the debt for those who trust in him so they would not perish under God's punishment, but have life with him fully and forever.[19] And that is only the beginning, since fixing man is the first part of fixing the world.

I want you to think for a moment about what that means. You can exchange your ponderous list of crimes, the heavy chains of guilt you forged in life, for the goodness of Christ. It is a gift, and the gift is free. It cannot be earned.[20] Jesus has already paid. It can only be received, humbly, on bended knee. You must simply trust him for it. And this is what the Story means by "faith."

CHAPTER 21

Trust

I HAVE SUGGESTED that the most remarkable rescue operation in history, the death of Jesus of Nazareth on a cross at Calvary, will do you no good unless you have faith. Nowadays, though, this is a dangerous thing to say because it is so easily misunderstood, so I must take a moment to clear up the confusion.

I, for one, am not fond of the English word *faith* (I will suggest a substitute in a moment). I think it has been corrupted for any productive use since it is too easy to mentally add the words *blind* or *leap of* to it. But that is not what the Story has in mind.

Christians are partly responsible for this confusion because they have not paid close attention to their own Story. But critics of Christianity have complicated the issue. Mark Twain might be forgiven for his well-known quip, "Faith is believing what you know ain't so," since he put the point in the mouth of one of his characters and might have been joking (though being a famous critic of religion, he might have meant it). Other critics seem to take the notion quite seriously, though.

The Skeptics Dictionary calls faith "a nonrational belief in some proposition." Others have said faith is pretending to know things you don't know or belief without evidence or the surrender of the mind and reason or belief in spite of the evidence—and various such things. This approach may be convenient for the superficial atheist, but it won't do for thoughtful people (atheist or otherwise) for a good reason.

If you want to critique a view, you must critique the view itself and not your own private version of it. Anyone is free, of course, to define faith according to his own fancy, but he is not free to import his fanciful definition into another's use of the word. If he does, he will be jousting with shadows and not the real thing—not the kind of "faith" the Story has in mind, at least. It is also not the way careful or polite people are supposed to make their point. Misrepresenting another person's view is not only bad thinking, it is bad manners.[1]

So here I must kindly insist that the critic of faith listen carefully. The Story knows nothing of what some people call "blind faith." Put this notion out of your mind completely since it is not a Christian concept—at least, not one promoted by Christians who understand the Story's view of faith, and that is the only view we are discussing here.

Consider, for example, these statements: "Jesus of Nazareth was a man *accredited by God to you by miracles, wonders and signs,* which God did among you through him, as you yourselves know" and "To these [apostles] he also presented himself alive after his suffering, *by many convincing proofs*, appearing to them over a period of forty days" and "Even though you do not believe me, *believe the works* [that is, the miracles], that you may know and understand that the Father is in me" and "Jesus did *many other signs* in the presence of his disciples, which are not recorded in this book. *But these are written that you may believe* that Jesus is the Messiah, the Son of God, and that by believing you may have life in his name."[2] You will find these kinds of claims throughout the Story from top to bottom.

Of course, anyone is free to assess the evidence itself, and some may find it wanting, but that is completely beside my point. It should be clear that the Story is not appealing to "nonrational belief" or "belief without evidence" or "surrender of the mind and reason" or "what you know ain't so." That is not the classical view of faith, even if some untutored Christians mistakenly hold it. In the Story, careful thinking and evidence matter, and there is a reason for this emphasis.

Before I explain the reason for the Story's emphasis on argument, evidence, and thoughtful deliberation, let me offer a suggestion that will prevent us from making a mistake. That mistake is thinking that *believing facts* and *having faith* are the same thing. They are not.

To avoid that problem, it might be helpful to treat the words *belief* and *faith* in different ways. We often use them interchangeably, of course, and this happens in the Story too. They are not always synonyms, however. There is a difference between "believing that" (what I want to now call "belief") and "believing in" (what we will now call "faith").

Here is the difference. The simple fact is, we may *believe that* something is true, but never *rely on it* for a single moment. We could be quite convinced, for example, that insulin injections will manage our diabetes, yet if we do not take our daily doses, our belief, though true, will do us no good. There is another step.

And here I want to suggest the substitute word I mentioned earlier that I think captures the Story's original meaning of *faith*. That word is *trust*, what ancient Christians called "*fiducia*." According to them, true faith was neither belief without knowledge (a "leap of faith"), nor a simple assent to certain truths ("believing that" Jesus was the Christ, for example). Rather, faith was knowledge in motion. It was "belief that" combined with "faith in"—active reliance, trust, in what they believed was true. Each was necessary. Neither was optional.[3]

Imagine, for a moment, you are planning a holiday in Europe. Your belief that airplanes and pilots and air traffic controllers make air travel possible will come in handy as a first step, but it will do you no good unless you eventually get onto an airplane. In the same way, faith requires belief, but it requires more than that. It requires action. It requires active trust.

The sad fact is, every Sunday, churches are filled with "believers" who are not Christians. There is nothing defective about their doctrine, yet they are still completely disconnected from God. They know *about* Jesus, they assent *to* Jesus, but they have never trusted *in* Jesus, and this is evident from the way they live their lives. Even in the Story many believed, after this fashion, but they never trusted. Judas comes immediately to mind.

At this point it is very easy to make a different mistake. I have said it is not enough simply to "believe." We must also trust. It turns out, though, that trust is not enough, either. There is another critical detail. We exercise trust, for example, when we climb on a plane bound for Paris. We entrust ourselves completely to the airplane and the pilot and the air traffic controllers. We are "all in," as it were. But our active faith itself takes us nowhere. It will never get us off the ground, into the air, and on to France. A capable pilot and plane must do that.

My point about a "capable pilot and plane" suggests the reason why the Story cares so much about argument, evidence, and thoughtful assessment.[4] Let me illustrate the issue by asking you a trick question (I'm warning you in advance because I want you to think about it before you answer). According to the Story, is a person saved by faith? To help you think carefully about the answer, consider this illustration.

Pretend for a moment you are a diabetic on the verge of a diabetic coma. Pretend also that I present you with a hypodermic syringe and a small vial that I tell you is insulin. Would you trust me to give you an injection to save your life?

The illustration shows a clear contrast between mere belief and active trust (the point I've just been making). You already believe that insulin can give you relief. But you remain in danger until you take a step of faith and actively entrust yourself to my care. So I suspect you might take me up on my offer.

If you did, however, you would be dead. Here's why: All the sincerity of your childlike trust could not change the fact that the vial in my illustration does not really contain insulin, only saline. You had both belief and faith, to be sure, but you would be dead, nonetheless.

Now that you know the trick, let me ask the same question again: Can a person be saved by *faith*? I think you realize now that the correct answer is no. Faith cannot save anyone, not even a Christian. Muslim suicide bombers overflow with authentic faith, but it does them no good. Trust can be misplaced, and often is.

Imagine a man venturing out on a frozen lake with complete confidence the ice is thick enough to hold his weight. However, if he is actually treading on thin ice you can instantly see that his bold faith will not protect him. In like manner, if you are taking a leap of faith trusting in a falsehood, your faith will do you no good no matter how strong your convictions may be. If you have an unshakable faith in something that turns out to be false, then you have an unshakable delusion, and the icy waters will soon get you.

If we are reaching out with the hand of faith to grasp a fantasy, then there will be no one there to rescue us, no matter how strong or sincere our faith is. No, faith does not save. Rather, *Jesus* saves *through* faith. He is the rescuer, and we reach for him, the "capable pilot."

This is why reason and evidence matter in the Story. It is critical to get certain facts right. Put simply—reason assesses, faith trusts.[5] That is the relationship of reason to faith. Reason helps us know what is actually true, leading to accurate belief. Faith is our step of trust to rely on what we have good reason to believe is so.

In one sense, then, Christianity is not based on faith at all. Rather, it is based on a Person we put our faith in. That means certain critical details about the Story must actually be true. The Story says, for example, that if Christians trust that Jesus rose from the dead, yet he did not—that is, if they believe in Jesus' resurrection contrary to fact—then their faith is futile. In this case, the Story says, believers should not be commended for their blind faith, but rather pitied for their foolishness.[6]

This relationship between faith and fact may be why Jesus had more to say about truth than he did about trust. He said that authentic worship had to be based on truth. He taught that walking in truth was the secret of genuine freedom from sin's enslaving power. He wanted his followers to be sanctified in truth through God's Word, which he said was the truth. He promised that everyone who valued truth would hear his voice. Indeed, Jesus was so filled with truth himself, he personally identified himself with it: "I am . . . the truth."[7]

Ancient Christians cared about getting the main things right. They knew the difference between merely believing something was true and actively relying on what they believed. They also knew their trust must be properly invested; their beliefs needed to be accurate. In fact, they felt so strongly about this they were willing to die (and did, in great numbers) for those things they believed to be true about Jesus of Nazareth.

If Jesus is not insulin, only saline, the Christian is lost in his sins no matter how strong or how genuine or how well-intended his faith is. So, unless the central details in the Story about Jesus are true *and* we actively trust in him, then Jesus will do us no good. We may go to church every week, but we will just be wasting our time.

Two more things. First, I fully realize there are some religious people who think that using the mind is the wrong approach to answering spiritual questions. They suggest that trusting feelings rather than careful reflection is the best guide to spiritual truth. This counsel often comes just after you are offered ideas that you should be inspecting carefully but are being told not to. It is like the used-car salesman who says, "Drive the car, but don't look under the hood." Yes, you may enjoy the ride for the moment, but you will never know if he is selling you a lemon or not.

The "trust your feelings" advice denies you the tools necessary to separate smart from foolish, wise from silly, safe from perilous. This is not good counsel since in life there are lots of lemons, and many of them are spiritually deadly. Never trust anyone who tells you to rely on experience over careful thinking. "Look before you leap" is sage advice. It applies especially to leaps of faith. Feelings are important. They make life beautiful. But careful thinking—reason—makes life safe.

Second, when you trust in Jesus, something else is happening at the same time. This step of trust marks a radical change in loyalties. There is a change of mind that results in a change of heart that results in a change of direction. This is trust in the deepest sense, not just trust *for something*, but trust *in Someone*, trust enough to follow faithfully in spite of the inconvenience. Like the prodigal son, you are returning to your Father.

The Story has a word for this turnaround. The word is *repentance*. It's not just religious lingo used by street preachers. It is central to the Story. Repentance involves a change of direction. You are turning from a life of selfishness and self-centeredness in which you (or other idols) are the center of everything to a life where God is the center and you (and everything else) are under him.

This turning means you will begin to live a different sort of life than you had been living before. As one has said, "To trust Him means, of course, trying to do all that he says. There would be no sense in saying you trusted a person if you would not take his advice."[8]

But we must not get our cart before our horse. There is a particular order to these things. You do not change the way you live in order to get on Jesus' path. Rather, getting on Jesus' path will change the way you live. Christ first catches his fish, then cleans them, the saying goes. Living the kind of life God wants us to live will not be possible until we get God's own life inside of us first. That happens when we take a step of trust.

And what exactly is it we are trusting Christ for? Two things, for the moment. First, that your sin went to Jesus' account and his goodness went to yours. Since Jesus was punished for your crimes against God, God is not angry at you anymore.[9] Indeed, he cannot be angry, since he has already poured every ounce of his anger on his Son. He is emptied of his wrath. He is satisfied.[10] This thought alone could transform your life, if you let it sink in. Second, you trust that God's own life inside of you will help you, day by day, to live as you ought. There are a great many more things you will trust him for, but they will come later. These two things will do for now.

What you choose to do about what happened at Calvary and on that first Easter morning with the empty tomb will make the deciding difference for you at the end of the Story. What is that difference? That question is answered with the final piece of our puzzle.

PART FIVE

RESURRECTION

CHAPTER 22

Four Facts

EVERY STORY OF REALITY has a theology, so to speak, even those stories that do not seem particularly religious. Those "theologies" represent the set of facts that cannot be dispensed with for the story to stay intact. Dickens's *A Christmas Carol* without Ebenezer Scrooge would no longer be the Christmas classic but some other tale.

The theology unique to our Story is minimally defined by two miracles that happened in history. I say "minimally" because there is so much more to the Story that is important, but if these two things were not in place then the Story simply would not hold together at all. I say "in history" because these miracles took place at a particular point in time and at a particular geographic location, and if that were not the case—if the miracles were only imaginative myths—they would do us no good.

The first miracle no one ever saw, because it could not be seen except by God alone. It is the trade between God the Father and God the Son that we have already spent some time thinking about. There was a second miracle, though, one relatively few witnessed, but multitudes have experienced. It happened three days after the trade, in the middle of the Jewish month of Nissan, in Palestine, in the spring of AD 33.[1]

When we think of the events that took place on what Christians call "Good Friday," there are reasons to take hope. That is why they call that particular Friday "good." But the death of Christ did not seem good to anyone at the time except, I guess, to the Jewish leadership and the Romans.

In *hindsight* the news is good, of course. On that Friday night, however, there were no poetic reflections on forgiveness, self-sacrifice, and slates wiped clean. There was just a bloody, brutally beaten corpse hanging from a cross. Jesus was dead. And he was taken down and he was buried. And the women were weeping and the men were hiding. And it was night and it was day and it was night again. And it all seemed over. And that was the end of it.

Then something remarkable happened. Exactly *what* happened has mystified historians. Whatever it was, it has changed everything.

Now, before I can tell you what historians, in the main, agree on regarding what actually happened those days and weeks following Jesus' execution, I would like to take a moment to dispatch three concerns that might muddy the process unless I address them.

In order to draw any conclusions about what happened at any point of history, one needs records, data, historical documents, and the like. The earliest and most thorough records of the life of Jesus—the ones credentialed historians themselves use for their studies—were written by Jesus' friends and followers who were in a position to give detailed information about the events of his life and death.[2] These documents are known as Matthew, Mark, Luke, and John.[3] Using these sources, though, raises concerns.

For one, some may suspect I will be subtly assuming these records of Jesus' life are reliable because they have been "divinely inspired," as Christians would put it—a "God said it, I believe it, that settles it" sort of thing. However, if that were my approach, I would be assuming something you might not assume, and my case for the resurrection of Jesus would not be persuasive.

So please hear me clearly. I do believe in the divine inspiration of the Story, true enough, but that has no bearing on the case for the resurrection I would like you to consider. You do not have to believe the documents are inspired in order to learn history from them. Since all the history that you and I think we know (and probably do know) comes from records written by ordinary people and not the hand of God, it ought to be clear we can do good history without bringing God into the discussion in that way.

Using the Gospels as source material for Jesus' life poses a second problem for some people. The writings, they suspect, cannot be trusted because they are biased. The authors were, after all, believers. They were already convinced about Jesus and, thus, had an agenda, a stake in the matter.

Of course, there is a point here, since there is little question the writers genuinely believed the story they told and, therefore, being "believers," had a personal interest in the issue. But is this really the liability some imagine it to be? The history of the Holocaust was written largely by its survivors. Should we doubt their accounts simply because these victims were also "believers" or because they had an "agenda," an intent to tell the world of this horrific event? I think not.

Regarding our Story, one might argue (ironically) that those Christians could be trusted *precisely because* they had a stake in the matter, in an odd sort of way—they staked their lives on the Story's accuracy. Who better to preserve the details of Jesus' life than those who knew him best, and who better to trust than those who put everything on the line—their homes, their families, their well-being—for their testimony about him?

Remember, bias can take two different forms. The first has just been mentioned—a point of view, an interest, an agenda. If dismissing reports for this reason were proper procedure, then the study of history would never get off the ground, since virtually everyone in a position to give accurate information has a "bias" of this sort. No, this kind of bias is largely benign on its own.

A problem arises only when a bias of the first sort leads to a bias of the second sort, that is, a tendency to distort or in some way misrepresent facts for personal gain. But what gain here? What advantage did these writers enjoy by fabricating a fake? Common sense tells us that men will not suffer martyrdom for myths they make up themselves.

In any event, having strong opinions about things that happened simply cannot, by itself, render a person's testimony about them unreliable, and historians know this. They are, of course, on the lookout for bias that distorts—and usually are able to root it out when it exists—but merely having an interest, or an experience, or a stake does not, on its own, disqualify. Those who suspect bias of the second sort must answer two important questions. First, what was the motive to lie or distort? Second, where is the evidence of the distortion? As far as I can tell, there was none of either in our Story.

Though the concern about bias is understandable and completely appropriate to raise, the complaint *as offered* is not adequate. The charge simply will not hold up unless there is convincing evidence of a *distorting* bias. That, to my knowledge, has never been demonstrated.

Finally, there are some who are tempted to think this entire approach is wrong-headed. In their view of things, a supernatural event could never be the best explanation for any evidence since supernatural stuff simply does not happen. We are, after all, talking about history, not religious fantasy. When it comes to the hard-core facts about things that happen in the real world, events like miraculous resurrections are simply out of bounds. We know better. This is the twenty-first century, after all, not the Middle Ages.

Well, I know of nothing that has been discovered in either history or science in the last hundreds of years that has rendered the idea of a man rising from the dead inherently implausible. Intellectual fashions have changed, true enough, but I hardly see what that has to do with matters of truth, since truth cares nothing for trends.

The impulse to reject the idea of a resurrection even before the evidence is examined does prompt a question, though. Why must we accept this constraint? I know it is a popular maneuver, but it strikes me as self-serving in a way that is not quite right. And here I need to remind you of a warning I offered earlier.[4] Certain details of one story will not be at home in a story of a different sort. If you disqualify the details of one worldview based on standards appropriate in a different kind of world, I think you will come perilously close to arguing in a circle. Would it not be best, rather, to simply follow the evidence where it leads instead of disqualifying certain options out of hand because the critic has a bias against them?

Here is the question I want you to consider. Do you want the *right* answers—that is, do you want to get clear on what actually happened that weekend in ancient Palestine—or do you merely want the *right kind* of answers, answers that fit your own agenda, regardless of evidence to the contrary? I think you can see the problem.

I recommend an open-minded approach. Shall we not let the facts speak for themselves? Remember, our task is uncovering reality. There are plenty of genuine obstacles to address already. Reality is challenging enough. Let us not stumble over obstacles of our own making that we arbitrarily place in our path.

So, how do historians recover the past? I am not a historian myself, but I have read enough about the process to know how the basic thing works. Good history is done in an indirect way (compared with the direct approach of other disciplines like, for example, chemistry) since no one has direct access to the events of time gone by. The past is past and that is that.

Instead, historians infer facts of the past based on evidence surviving in the present—written documents of different kinds, archaeological finds, assorted artifacts, and the like. Thus, historians do not trade in proofs, but in probabilities. Their craft is not mechanical, like math or logic, but more of an art, like detective work—following leads, assessing clues, weighing scenarios, seeking the best explanation given all the evidence, and so on. And that is the goal, of course—determining the most probable account of what took place in light of all the relevant information.

Some types of evidence are more valuable to historians than others, though. Multiple, independent sources have more weight than solitary references, and the closer in time to the event the better. Eyewitness accounts will be superior to second-hand ones. Embarrassing admissions add weight to a testimony. After all, who would invent a detail that makes him or his case look bad? And if an antagonist affirms a fact that actually helps his opposition, then it adds credibility to the point. And so forth. As it turns out, scholars have known for a long time that the Gospels fare exceptionally well when put to these sorts of tests.[5]

So now to our question. What would it take to show that a person actually, truly rose from the dead? I guess the simplest approach would be to show, first, that a person was dead at one point in time and, second, that the same person was alive at a later point in time. And if some considerable time had passed—say, days later as opposed to minutes later—all the better. That, it seems to me, would do the job.

Of course, the person must be truly dead, not just passed out or not just *nearly* dead like some people whose bodies quit on them for a while for some reason (sickness, accident, trauma) and their souls go away somewhere for a bit and then return. That won't do. No, the person would have to be really, truly, dead-as-a-doornail dead.

So what do the historical facts show in the case of Jesus? On this issue there is safety in numbers. Though occasional exceptions pop up, as a general rule when an overwhelming number of scholars agree to a certain set of facts—especially when their reasons for agreement are good ones—we may proceed with confidence. And that is what we will do.

Nowadays, the vast majority of scholars on the life of Jesus—including those who are entirely secular and have no religious stake in the matter—agree to four facts of history. First, Jesus died on a Roman cross on Friday and was buried in a tomb. Second, that tomb was empty Sunday morning. Third, numerous witnesses testified—at great peril to themselves—that they saw Jesus alive multiple times after he had died, that they met with him and even ate with him. Finally, even the skeptic, James, and the mortal enemy of Christians, Saul of Tarsus, were convinced they had seen Jesus risen from the dead, and both willingly died rather than recant—James stoned, and Paul beheaded.[6]

Now, when I say these four facts represent the overwhelming consensus of professional historians specializing in the life of Jesus, even the skeptical ones, I am speaking quite literally. The conclusion is the result of an exhaustive analysis surveying 1,400 academic sources published since 1975, printed in English, French, and German.[7] Another work lists twelve commonly accepted facts,[8] but these four will do for now.

Let me say outright that most scholars do not think Jesus rose from the dead. No, there is a split decision on this question. But here is the curious thing. Most of those same critics, on the main, reject every one of the standard naturalistic explanations for our facts too, explanations that, if they were sound, would favor their own view. This means, first, the evidence against those alternatives must be very good indeed. Second, it raises a question. If most scholars agree that natural explanations are simply not adequate, then why not consider a supernatural explanation that makes sense of all the evidence? Why would a real resurrection not do?

Well, you must ask them, I suppose, but it seems to me it is best, as I mentioned, to follow the facts themselves and see where they most likely lead. Thoughtful people are careful to stay open to all the options and not jump to conclusions in one direction or the other.

These facts of history are within our reach. After all, the evidence itself is not supernatural, but earthly—a corpse of a crucified man, a tomb that is empty, testimonies of encounters, radical and complete reversals of convictions—things any mortal has access to for investigation. And what could be amiss if we infer as the most probable explanation of those facts that a man rose from the dead, especially if every rival explanation seems wholly implausible (as I will show in a moment)? Facts are what they are, and they often lead without incident to obvious conclusions. Why not follow?

Here is what we are looking for: a single explanation that makes sense of all of the agreed-upon facts taken together. It is the way we solve most problems in life, and I do not see why the same approach will not serve us well in this situation.

If someone is determined to stick to biases instead of facts, then there is not much I have to say to him. He is stumbling over an obstacle he has placed in the way himself, and we may ask why he thinks this approach is sound.

Our four facts are the bedrock, so to speak, the starting point for historians, and for good reason. Each is fully supported by the kind of evidence (mentioned above) that makes any historical claim trustworthy.

For example, there is no question that Jesus was dead. The Romans killed him. He'd been brutally beaten, whipped, fastened to a cross with nails in hands and feet, exposed naked all afternoon in the April air, speared through his chest, then declared dead by a battle-seasoned Roman centurion.[9] He'd been embalmed with over eighty pounds of chemicals,[10] and his body was stretched out on a slab of rock and sealed in a cold crypt.

So our first step to resurrection is in place. Jesus was truly dead at one point in time. That is the first fact. The remaining three facts that scholars agree on address the second concern. Was Jesus, at some later point in time, truly alive?

Two-thirds to three-quarters of all scholars in the field agree that Jesus' tomb was empty. It is easy to see why. There is no record of any kind that the empty tomb was ever disputed by anyone, even those who had Jesus executed in the first place. Corpses decay more slowly in the arid environment of Palestine. Jesus' body could still probably be identified even after decomposing for more than a month.[11] Why did no one produce the remains and end the controversy? Present the corpse, end the issue. But there was no body.

Some at the time did claim the disciples stole the body,[12] and there are those today who think that might have happened. But does that seem likely to you? Note, first, the charge is a clear admission by enemies of Jesus that there was no body. More to the point, what good would it do the disciples to steal Jesus' remains, then lie about a resurrection? The basic rule with lying is this: Invent a story that benefits you, not one that gets you beaten, whipped, stoned, crucified upside down, or beheaded. My personal view is that any skeptic who is attracted to that explanation is simply not skeptical enough. Anyway, virtually no scholar today defends this notion.[13]

And what of the appearances? The disciples were clearly convinced they had met the risen Christ, a detail so historically certain, one called it, "virtually indisputable and therefore undisputed."[14] Even exceedingly critical scholars admit the disciples *thought* they saw Jesus, but *what* had they actually seen?

You might think they *imagined* they saw Christ, but didn't really. That certainly is possible in individual cases, and it is the going theory at the moment. That's because people imagine things all the time, and some even hallucinate. But how exactly would that work in this case? It is hard to believe that so many different people—even complete skeptics—in different locations, at different times, as individuals and in groups, over more than a month, could have had the same hallucination about the same person who they all were quite certain (for good reason) had been killed and buried just days or weeks before.

And here I want you to note something many people miss when considering this option. Hallucinations are entirely private experiences, just like dreams. People imagine things, after all, in their imaginations. You might tell someone about your vision or your apparition or your hallucination or whatever, but they cannot join you in it, even if they wanted to (which doubters like James and Saul certainly did not). Since these kinds of delusions are in someone's head, so to speak, and not, say, in the room or at the seashore or on the mountaintop, they cannot be shared with those standing about, especially if the onlookers are skeptical to begin with.

Do you see the problem? If it is unlikely you can wake your wife and invite her to share in a particularly pleasant dream you just enjoyed, it is equally unlikely the disciples shared a common hallucination, multiple times over, no less. For my part, I am quite confident I know the difference between a dream and reality, and I wager you do too. I suppose the disciples did as well, especially when their lives depended on it.

No, imagining a risen Jesus will not do as an explanation. Anyhow, even if it were somewhat plausible (which it is not), this alternative does nothing to explain the empty tomb and the missing body, so it cannot really be in the running. You can see why so many scholars are skeptical of this alternative.

It looks as if we are running out of options. Only one remains, one reasonable explanation for all the facts—the death of Jesus, the empty tomb, the appearances to the disciples, the conversion of the skeptics.

What would transform a group of shivering, shaking, terrified men who had abandoned Jesus—one even denying he knew him—scattered, hiding from the authorities, doors locked, lights out? What could account for their transformation into bold advocates for the resurrection, standing up to authorities who threatened to scourge, imprison, and execute them for declaring a risen Christ?

What would change Saul of Tarsus, a man so dedicated to his religion he rounded up men and women to be bullied, beaten, and killed for following Jesus? What would cause such a man to turn on a dime and take his place with those he oppressed, eventually sacrificing his own life for the very Gospel he previously despised? What best explains that?

Only one answer will do. It is the answer given by the one who had earlier renounced Christ with an oath. In Peter's words, "This Jesus, God raised up again, to which we are all witnesses."[15]

And if risen, then Jesus is the Son of God, because he was declared to be so "with power by the resurrection from the dead." And if risen, we have been forgiven because "He who was delivered over for our transgressions . . . was raised because of our justification." And if risen, we now have no condemnation because Jesus "who was raised, who is at the right hand of God . . . intercedes for [us]."[16]

And because Jesus has risen, there will be another resurrection when he returns at the end of the Story—the first securing the second—the great raising of all humanity for the final chapter, the final resolution—where all brokenness is repaired, all evil is vanquished, and all beauty is restored.

CHAPTER 23

In Between

WE ARE NEARLY AT THE END of our Story, but first we need to go back to the beginning of our conversation to put the ending in its proper perspective.

Early on I mentioned there was one thing virtually everyone agreed on when they thought about the world they lived in. Everyone was convinced something had gone terribly wrong. Indeed, that fact is so obvious it is one of the biggest reasons many are skeptical of the Story to begin with.

I told you then that the brokenness of the world was not the problem for Christianity that people thought it was, since evil was actually part of our Story. It wasn't part of the very beginning, of course, because when God put everything together at the first there was no evil. All was just as he wanted it, just the way it was supposed to be, everything fulfilling its proper purpose, everything completely good.

Evil intruded later when man rebelled and broke the world. Indeed, without that unfortunate failing, there would be no Story at all. Every story, after all, is about fixing something that's gone wrong—an endeavor thwarted, an adventure gone awry, a relationship ruined. Our Story is the same way. It is about how God takes a broken world and broken people and puts everything back together again. It is about how the Story's conflict gets resolved and how fallen people get restored. That is why I reminded you early on that our Story was not over yet.

•

I also spoke of a different concern, a different kind of objection, the complaint about Jesus being the only solution to man's problem and, therefore, the only way to repair our friendship with God. Initially, such a claim seemed ridiculously narrow. But we learned there was a good reason for it. Jesus is the only way back home because he is the only one who solved the problem.

The world went bad because man went bad first. Since man's brokenness broke the world, and only Jesus is able to heal man's moral injury, he is the only One who can heal the world's injury too. These two things are tied together. Put another way, Jesus, the God-man, is man's only hope because only Jesus can fix the problem of evil. Only God coming down into the world can rescue the world from itself.

As in all stories, though, the final restoration does not come quickly. Complex problems are not swiftly solved. There are plot details that must be played out. That delay is often difficult to endure.

When a mother loses her child to a deadly disease, the grief is unbearable and a single question presses relentlessly: Why? It is the same question each of us asks in the difficult circumstances of our lives. Why? Why at this time? Why me, or this child, or this friend, or this neighbor, or that innocent person on the other side of the world? Why?

Part of this question cannot be answered since it is beyond human knowledge. Why does any particular soldier, for example, take a particular bullet, on a particular spot, on a particular battlefield? These are secret things known to God alone,[1] and he keeps his own counsel on them.

Another part of this question is not so difficult, though. It is something the Story reminds us of often. We all live between the beginning of the Story and its end, and that is dangerous territory. From the moment of that terrible fall, the human race has been in the grip of a terrible conflict. A war rages, and every war has its battles, and every battle has its casualties. This we know.

We also know this war will have an end because the Author himself has told us it will. The end of the war is the end of the Story. There will be a victory. The evil will be punished. The wounds will be mended. The tears will be wiped away. The world will be made right again.

For now, though, we endure for mercy's sake—God's mercy. This may seem like an odd thing for me to say, but this too makes sense when you understand the Story. Human rebellion broke the world, and with human disobedience comes human guilt. Our prints—yours and mine—are on the smoking gun. We are deeply in debt to God, and the debt must be paid. Either we pay or Another pays for us. That is the arithmetic we have already discussed.

Some will never seek mercy, but many will. Not everyone who will ask forgiveness from God, though, has done so. God's delay is not due to slowness, then, or to powerlessness or to lack of pity. Rather, God is waiting. He delays because of patient compassion.[2] When the final curtain falls, he knows the play will be over. When evil is defeated, it will be defeated completely. The time for mercy will have run out. Justice will have its day and multitudes will feel its force.

In the meantime, those who trust him are not alone in the struggle, even though we take casualties. He is with us, always, in everything. That is his promise.[3] "In the world you have tribulation," Jesus told us, "but take courage. I have overcome the world."[4]

And here we must ask ourselves a question about the solution to it all. It is normal to wonder why God doesn't do something to end the trouble. But precisely what would you like him to do? I suspect you would want him to give the bad people their comeuppance and then fix things so this kind of mess could never happen again. Well, that is precisely what is going to take place. But this will not be good news for everyone.

We are coming to the part of our Story that tells us what will happen at the end of this great battle the world has been in. Since what we are about to discuss concerns the future, it is the part we know least about. Even so, it is both the most popular and the most unpopular part of the Story.

The little we know about how the Story ends is both thrilling and terrifying, depending. Some things you will learn are wonderful beyond description. Other things I am about to tell you are so chilling they can take your breath away when you realize the weight of them. If it makes you frightened, that's okay. It's right to be afraid of something truly dangerous. And for many people, the future is very dangerous indeed.

The first thing you need to know is that in this Story everyone will live forever—you and me, our friends and our loved ones, strangers and enemies. Every person who has ever lived will always continue to live for all time. In a certain sense, then, you have never met a "mere" mortal.[5] Their lives, once begun, will never end.

But living forever will not be good news for all, because in this story not everyone lives happily ever after. At that final event of history as we know it, one of two things will take place: perfect justice or perfect mercy.[6] Perfect justice—punishment for everything we have ever done wrong, and God misses nothing—or perfect mercy—forgiveness for everything we have ever done wrong, and God misses nothing.

CHAPTER 24

Perfect Justice

HAVE YOU EVER WONDERED why so many people seem to "get away with murder," as some would put it, why so many terrible crimes and malicious acts and gratuitous injustices seem to pass without consequence? Don't you sometimes feel, deep down inside, a kind of hunger for those accounts to be balanced? Don't you occasionally long that justice will someday be done? I think there is something good in all of us that wants to see the wrongs of the world righted.

Do not despair. That time will come. The first step to fixing what has gone wrong with the world is to punish the people who have done the wrong. The guilty will not escape, not in the final accounting. There will be a day of reckoning, and those who cheated justice in this life will one day feel the penalty that is theirs to bear.

This is good news in one sense, but it is very bad news in another. Others will get their comeuppance, quite right, but we will be standing before the same judge, since we each have our own crimes to answer for.

And here we must be careful to avoid a common mistake. Apparently, most people—in America, at least—believe in hell, yet the majority of them are convinced they will not be going there. They think they are "basically good," or at least good enough to escape the fate that awaits lesser men. But they will be mistaken.

I told you in an earlier part of our discussion[1] that in the final chapters of the Story there is a scene where certain books are opened. These different books signal different ends. I said that every sinful act of every person who ever lived—a complete list of every crime that anyone has ever committed against God[2]—has been recorded in these books. None of the terrible things you were afraid people had gotten away with have been missed. The record will be plain for all to see, and each deed will be answered for. But each of the abysmal things you have done—things you hoped no one would ever find out about—are written there, too. They will be answered for, as well.

The record in the books is the "certificate of debt" I mentioned before, our record of wrongs—our "rap sheets," so to speak. Some lists will appear modest compared to others; some will seem endless. For each person, though, his own list—whether long or short by our reckoning—will still overwhelm him. These are the Books of Death.

Like Jacob Marley,[3] we wear the chains we forged in life, link by link and yard by yard. These books record the ponderous weight of them, the sins each of us bear, even though amusements in life may have temporarily distracted us from their heaviness.

The Books of Death will be opened by One with wounds in his hands and feet, and a gash in his side. This Jesus who is the world's only Savior will also be the world's final judge.[4] It is his second appearance before man. He came first in mercy, to liberate and to save.[5] The second time will be different. At his final coming, Jesus distributes death. The Story says:

> Then I saw a great white throne and him who was seated on it. The earth and the heavens fled from his presence, and there was no place for them. And I saw the dead, great and small, standing before the throne, and books were opened. Another book was opened, which is the Book of Life. The dead were judged according to what they had done as recorded in the books. . . . Anyone whose name was not found written in the Book of Life was thrown into the lake of fire.[6]

This is a sobering scene, and some may think I am now trying to scare them. If so, they would be right. I am. As I mentioned earlier, it is good to be frightened by something truly dangerous. I hope you will not think I am merely using a scare *tactic*, though, a ruse to coerce people into compliance. This is not what I am doing. This is not subterfuge. Rather, it is truth told in order to warn.

All who stand before that throne will be judged according to their own behavior, their conduct while on earth, and they will all be found wanting. No unrepentant criminal will get away with anything in the long run.

But there is another book, the Book of Life. It also contains a record, the names of those who, though guilty, have received mercy, at their request: "God, be merciful to me, a sinner." All those who have accepted their pardon in Christ will be absolved.

So all human beings will be raised from the dead never to die again. Some will be raised to eternal life. But others will be raised to eternal death. The spiritually alive will never perish because of Jesus' trade. Their names are written in the Book of Life. The spiritually dead will remain forever spiritually dead, the price of their own crimes recorded in the Books of Death. Put another way, there is not a crime against God that does not go unpunished, and there is not a crime against God that cannot—because of the Rescuer—be forgiven. Centuries ago, John Newton, the author of the hymn "Amazing Grace," put it this way: "I am a great sinner; and Christ is a great Savior."

Let me tell you three things you need to know about hell, other than that it's real. The first is this. Hell is a place of banishment from God's presence. The Story says, "These will pay the penalty of eternal destruction, away from the presence of the Lord and from the glory of his power . . ."[7]

Many people in this life simply want nothing to do with God, and they are happy to say so. To be near him would be agony, they think, so they don't care much (at the moment) if they are kept from him forever. They think this will give them a kind of freedom. They have lived their lives entirely on their own without his interference, and they would be quite content to keep it that way. That is their will and, in the end, they shall have what they want. To those, God will say, "Depart."

But thinking this way is a fatal mistake. Banishment from God will not be the pleasant experience some have imagined. God himself is the source of all things good—all pleasures, all joys, all satisfactions, all comforts. Everything wonderful you have ever experienced came from him.[8] Even if you have never believed in God, he has still been good to you. All the pleasures of this life are only possible because he is gracious, even to unbelievers. But that will not last, because to be banished from his presence is to be denied every goodness that makes any enjoyment possible.

Notice how the Story describes the banishment. It calls it "eternal destruction." This does not mean you will disappear, as some suggest. Things that are destroyed do not vanish. They are simply ruined for their purpose. The same will happen to those who are lost. They will not vanish—everyone lives forever. Rather, they will be forever ruined for their original purpose. You were made for happiness with God, and without him you will be denied any goodness of any kind. And that will be unspeakable agony. That will be hell.

So that is the first thing we must see clearly. There can be no happiness without God, only anguish. Which brings me to the second thing you need to know about hell. It is a place of unspeakable torment.

Jesus spoke of outer darkness with weeping and gnashing of teeth because of the intolerable suffering.[9] He told of a man in Hades who was in such torment, he begged that a drop of water be touched to his tongue to ease his agony in the flames.[10]

Now, you may debate whether there is real fire in hell or not, but that is hardly the point. I, for one, am not convinced about literal flames or darkness or gnashing teeth. Sometimes eternal things are described in earthly terms because no other options are available. What I am completely convinced of, though, is that the suffering is real and severe, whatever images may be pressed into play to describe it.

Here is the final thing you need to know about hell, and it is probably the most unsettling of all. The conscious torment and suffering of those banished by God will never end. Ever.

It is tempting to think that forever is a long, long time, but that would not be accurate. Anything with a length has an end to it, and even a long, long time runs its course, eventually. Hell does not, and that is difficult to imagine.

Everything in our lives has an ending. Our day comes to an end, we rest for the night, then start over the next day. The school term comes to an end, we vacation for a bit, then start another term. Eventually our lives come to an end, and that's usually the farthest forward we reach with our minds. If you try to think for a moment as far into the future as you possibly can—however far ahead your thoughts can take you—you will not have even started your journey into eternity.

When I try, I can imagine living hundreds of years, maybe, but even then my mental reach still comes to rest somewhere in the distant future. If I try to go further, if I try to imagine there is no end at all, if I try to imagine going on forever and ever, I begin to feel something like a panic inside, like I am falling from a high tower but never ever landing anywhere, just falling and falling. I don't know what you feel when you think about forever, but it is not a pleasant experience for me.

But now change one detail. You will not be falling forever; you will be suffering forever. Jesus said hell was like Gehenna, where "their worm does not die, and the fire is not quenched."[11] Gehenna was a place his listeners knew well, the dump outside the walls of Jerusalem where the refuse of the city—the trash, the garbage, the discarded waste, the cast-offs, even decaying corpses—smoked and smoldered continuously, and worms and maggots fed on it without end. His words were figurative, of course (I do not think there are worms in hell), but the everlasting punishment Jesus spoke of is very real.

One writer put it this way: "When a damned soul shall have shed tears enough to fill all the rivers of the world, even if he should shed but one a century, he will be no nearer deliverance after so many millions of years; he will only have begun to suffer."[12]

Hell will be like that. There will be no escape. You will never be released. You will never disappear. And the suffering will never end, ever. The clock will never stop ticking. In fact, the clock will never even start.

And here I anticipate a complaint. How is an eternal hell an example of a loving God? Well, the one who raises the issue is on to something. Hell is not an example of God's love. It is an example of his justice. His love is demonstrated by his free offer of pardon from hell, which many decline. But they will not be able to decline his justice.

The question in some ways reflects a misunderstanding, though. To say, "God is love" is not the same as saying, "Love is God." Those are very different statements. God and love are not identical, though this seems to be what some people think. They think that saying, "God is love" is all there is to say about God, that love and God are one and the same, and there is nothing further to talk about.

It is correct to say God is love, if you are very careful with your meaning. Love is a true attribute of God, but he is more than just love. Other qualities are essential to God, too. One of them is justice. Wrongs must be punished; debts must be paid.

In fact, in a very real sense, God's love and his justice go together. Think of it this way. We all know that God would not be God—that is, he would not be the most perfect Being imaginable—if he were not also good. God's goodness and his love are kin to each other, so to speak, because God's goodness and his love spring from the same source—his perfect nature.

But the same is true of God's justice. If God let wicked people simply go free, then he would not be good at all. And if he were not good, it is very difficult to see how he could be loving. Since God's love and justice are both good things, they are not in conflict with each other.

If you still insist that a loving God would never send anyone to hell, then you must settle in your mind that desperately evil acts will forever remain unpunished. God will simply "look the other way" when evil is done, as if nothing had happened. That is what you must accept. Yet isn't part of our complaint about evil that evil people get away with the evil they have done? Have you thought about what that would mean?

For example, I once heard a talk given by a man who had been so brutalized by his captors he could no longer stand up to give his address, so he spoke to his audience while seated. Here is what he wrote in his memoirs:

The communist torturers often said, "There is no God, no Hereafter, no punishment for evil. We can do what we wish. . . . I thank God, in whom I don't believe, that I have lived to this hour when I can express all the evil in my heart." He expressed it in unbelievable brutality and torture inflicted on prisoners.[13]

But there is something else, and this may be what you have been getting at with your complaint. God is also merciful, and that must be factored into the equation, you say. Quite right, and here is how it fits in. God's mercy is also kin to his goodness, just like his love. God is not *obliged* to show mercy, of course. No one is owed forgiveness, just as no criminal is owed a pardon. Mercy is "above and beyond," so to speak. It is an overflow of God's goodness that makes mercy possible.

You see where I am going with this. I am trying to show you that there is no contradiction between God's love, which is wonderful, and God's justice, which is terrifying. I want you to see that they come together in a breathtaking way when his love and his justice and his mercy all converge at a cross. "God is the only comfort," Lewis has written. "He is also the supreme terror: the thing we most need, and the thing we most want to hide from."[14]

But there is still one other part to this objection, isn't there? It is the part that I said was the most unsettling thing of all about hell—the "forever" part, the suffering that will never end, ever. "Isn't that a bit much?" you may be thinking. "Yes, there is a legitimate point about justice—about people not getting away with murder and God not looking the other way and criminals getting their due and accounts being balanced and all that. But does not justice itself require a limit? Where is the justice in a sentence of eternal torment for sins committed in a moment of time?"

Let me say at the outset that I am sympathetic to this concern since I have felt it myself. In those panicked moments I spoke of, I too wonder about the equity of everlasting damnation. There are three things, though, that caution me against trusting my own sensibilities on this.

First, the ones who are guilty are not in the best position to assess the gravity of their own crimes. Our moral senses, though intact, are still marred by our own rebellion. We simply do not see our sin for what it is. Virtually every person in prison considers himself unfairly penalized. It should not be surprising when we feel the same way with our own crimes against God.

Second, the proper punishment for an offense is never proportionate to the amount of time it took to commit it. A burglary can be accomplished by a clever crook in a matter of minutes, an act of murder in a split second. Though the second is the greater crime, it takes less time to carry out. No, the gravity of an offense is not measured by anything temporal, but by something else, and that is my third point.

The severity of a wrong is not determined solely by the act itself, but also by the one against whom the wrong was committed. An illustration might help here. Let us imagine that your child has blackened the eye of a schoolmate without good reason. This would be an act he must answer for, no question. But now suppose your child gave the same black eye to you, his parent. This is something else, isn't it. The attack upon you is clearly the more egregious offense, even though the behavior itself is exactly the same thing done to the schoolmate.

Now, the point is this. When we sin, we are not sinning against a schoolmate or a teacher or a parent or an earthly king. We are morally assaulting the Sovereign of the universe whose own moral purity is perfect. What could be just recompense for a crime such as this? Here I think the unending banishment fits, as troublesome as it seems to our own sensibilities.

In the end, it all comes down to this. One day you will stand before God, who will sit in judgment on your life, and you will be found guilty. I suspect you already know that. When that time comes for you—and it will come—only one thing will save you from the punishment that is your due—God's Rescuer, Jesus.

Here is the Story's solution to the problem of evil: perfect justice for evildoers, perfect mercy for the penitent; evil banished forever, and everlasting good restored.

CHAPTER 25

Perfect Mercy

WE ARE EACH BORN with a deep hunger that haunts us our entire life. Its satisfaction stays beyond our reach, even though we are promised, by the rulers of this world, that the right amusements or the right possessions or the right relationships or the right experiences will put this longing to rest. We have been told that the things our hearts long for can be found on this earth, in this lifetime. But we have been misled.

We soon discover that those things will never give us what we really want because we have been made for another world, and the thing we long for, even ache for—the Story calls it a kind of groaning[1]—is not to be found in this world or in this lifetime. We have been longing for home, and for a Father who waits for us there, and we are lonely here in exile until we are finally together with him.

God's perfect mercy—forgiveness for everything we have ever done wrong—means we will finally, one day, be going home, and finally, one day, our hunger will be satisfied.

Before I say much more about this, though, I must first pause to confess a certain personal limitation. I face a difficulty here similar to the one I encountered earlier in this book. I struggled then to give you an awareness of what a "just right" world looked like at the very beginning of the Story before the world was ruined by human foolishness. Here I face the same challenge, trying to describe what a perfect world will be like when this broken realm is remade, when all of our memories of woe fade to nothingness, and all our anguish and dissatisfactions are replaced with incandescent happiness.

Part of the difficulty is this: it is much easier for people to believe in heaven than for them to believe in hell (for obvious reasons, I think), but it is much harder for them to envision heaven than to envision hell. Vice is always much less difficult to portray than virtue, so our sense of hell has a vividness that our sense of heaven cannot match. The hellish images are easy to grasp because we are well acquainted with suffering. Heaven, though, lies largely beyond our mental reach.

I suspect hell will probably be a lot more like people have been told than most are willing to believe. Heaven, on the other hand, will probably be little like we picture it—at least as I picture it, and maybe it's the same for you. At the end of the Story we read descriptions that do not resonate well with modern ears[2]—a massive, cubic, heavenly city with pearly gates and streets of gold, walls shining with the brilliance of jasper, and a river, clear as crystal, flowing from a throne nourishing a tree of life that bears fruit for the healing of nations. Frankly, since I personally care little for great estates, jewelry, or thrones, this picture leaves me somewhat flat.

Please understand, I am not finding fault with the Divine revelation. The fault is entirely my own, imprisoned as I am for the moment in my fallen self. The truth is, there is a mercy that awaits us that is so wonderful it is difficult for us to get our minds around, being sullied, as we are, by our trek in this fallen world and weighed down by its woes. At my best I can offer you nothing, I am afraid, but the faintest glimpse of Glory because that is all I have myself.

We know this, though. We were made for something far better than what we experience in this life. And we long for it. It is, as C. S. Lewis put it, a "desire for our own far-off country."[3] That country is ours, an inheritance reserved for us by our King,[4] but we have not yet reached it, and it is hard to lay hold of precisely how it will be.

To repair this breech, I find it more helpful to dwell on what heaven will *be* like rather than on what it will *look* like (which I suspect is the point of the elegant imagery in the first place, though its impact escapes me personally). Along the way in the Story, we are told things that give us glimpses, however faint they may be compared to the reality of heaven itself, and that is where I would like to offer some thoughts.

God's perfect mercy will change everything for us, of course, but let me try to describe just a few of the things the Story tells us about the future for followers of the Rescuer.

Here is the first thing I want you to think about. When a person has always been dirty, it is hard for him to know what it might feel like to be completely clean. Even though sometimes he is not quite as dirty as other times, he is always grimy and soiled in some measure. He has never known the refreshment that hot water, soap, and a good scrub can provide.

We are in a similar situation. The *fact* is we are completely clean before God because of the trade I spoke of earlier, but the *feeling* of purity eludes us. Most of us have never, ever felt completely clean since our contact with our own sin every day—and our memories of the sins of our past—sully our sense of absolution, and it shames us. Maybe some great saints have felt unsoiled sometimes, but I never have.

This is why it is a sensible practice to remind ourselves of the fact of our Father's faithful mercy—what the ancient Hebrews called his "loving-kindness"—when our feelings tell us otherwise.

The Story does this often.[5] It says things like, "And their sins and their lawless deeds I will remember no more," and, "Though your sins are as scarlet, they will be as white as snow. Though they are red like crimson, they will be like wool," and, "You were washed, you were sanctified, you were justified in the name of the Lord Jesus Christ." And many other wonderful encouragements such as these. The sounds of these words wash over our souls, comforting us, reminding us of a purity that, because of Jesus, we possess before God, but because of failings, we seldom feel ourselves.

When we finally go home, though, we will not need reminders. Purity will penetrate us so completely we will feel nothing else—no guilt, no defilement, no pain of moral brokenness, no shame.

I hesitate to use the word holiness here since it suggests (unfortunately) not plenitude, but privation—a denial of pleasure for the seemingly leaner satisfactions of virtue. But holiness is the right word, and it does not mean privation, but abundance, sweet goodness without limit. And when we are home, we will be immersed in it, filled with it, soaked in it—thoroughly good, yet still, remarkably, ourselves.

The Story says, "When Christ appears, *we shall be like him*, for we shall see him as he is."[6] We will be good because he is good. We will be holy because he is holy. We will be transformed to be as he is.[7]

This is the first wonder. Mercy makes it so.

And here we come to another wonder tied to the first. The reason there will be no guilt, no defilement, no brokenness or shame for us—no sense of sin—is because there will be no sin, ours or others, anywhere. Evil will be banished, forever, never to return. Nothing and no one to harm us, and no one we will harm. Our tears will be dried by God himself,[8] our wounds healed, our anguish ended. Our souls will be safe, comforted, and at rest.

The Story says death will be abolished and there will be no night,[9] only the light of Glory surrounding us. All the results of the bad and all of the enemies of the good will be no more. The afflictions we feel in this life, as unbearable as they sometimes seem, will shrink to insignificance in light of an eternal weight of Glory[10] that will be ours in abundance.

Here is the reason we will always be safe from sin. Earlier we learned that our badness made the world go bad, that the world is broken because we are broken. This will never happen again, because we will never be broken inside again. When the Maker makes all things new—the New Heaven, the New Earth,[11] you, me, everyone, everything all overflowing with goodness—we will not have the kind of goodness we had before, the kind that could falter, the kind that could fail. Jesus has purchased a different purity for us—his own—and has given it to us in the trade. Jesus' goodness, God's own goodness, perfect goodness. Not as something we possess, but as something we *are*. Not attached to us, but rather the full Glory of God's own goodness now *built into us* so we never fall short of it again.[12] We will be free to do as we wish, since our every desire, like God's, will be good and pure and right.

So, in the resurrection there will be no broken world because there will be no broken people because there will be no sinners. Mercy makes it so.

The resurrection will not only change our insides, it will change our outsides, as well. There will be no broken bodies. Now I hope you will not think this simply means the backache will be gone, the epilepsy will be cured, or the lame will run like the wind, though that would be wonder enough. Yes, all of the physical brokenness will be fixed, no question, but I think that is the smaller part of the matter. I suspect the transformation will be so magnificent, even the healthiest among us will have seemed physical wretches compared to our new heavenly selves.

Our bodies will be remade, not just mended. They will be completely new since the bodies we have now are not suited for heaven.[13] They will still be our own bodies, of course, recognizable as ourselves,[14] but still so different even the writers of the Story struggled, at times, to give us a glimpse of what the Glory of that newness will be like.[15] We are so used to the physical burdens of this world that it is impossible for us to imagine the lightness of being we will experience when those burdens are lifted.

This is our significant resurrection, not that our bodies will be made whole again—though they will be whole in a way they never could be in this life—but that our whole *selves* will be changed and transformed, new and perfect, suited for a new and perfect place.

And here is another mercy. I want you to imagine if you can—and if you are a Christian—all of the genuine believers you have ever known who are no longer alive. Think of parents or grandparents, spouses or children, close friends or casual companions, many you loved deeply, some taken slowly, painfully, others swiftly—violently even—before their time. They were yours and now they are gone.

When friends and relatives stand by a graveside at funerals mourning and remembering, I know it is a polite thing to say, "They are in a better place," or "You will see them again." But this is not true of everyone. Many do not go to a better place and they will never be seen again. That is a dark promise God has made that we have already discussed.

But God has made another promise as well. Those under his mercy are not gone forever. There will be a reunion. You will be together with them again. And not like before with pain of past hurts or competition or infighting polluting your attachments. There will be none of the negatives that now sully even the best of friendships. Rather, it can truly be said you will know them at their very best, enjoying a feast of togetherness with them without end.

No, your close ones in the Lord are not lost, like others. You will be with them. The Story tells us so, comforting us now, while we wait.[16]

And there is so much more, but that would take more books and more vision than is in me. This will have to do for now, and even in what I have told you I've faltered, as I warned. Our own imaginations cannot take us very far, supplied, as they are, with images from this life that do not befit the life to come. I have offered the faintest of sketches, a child's scrawl, a pale resemblance to future Glory. Words can scarcely give you a glimpse. They can only point you in the direction of the sunrise. But it is the best I can do for now.

Except for this.

Have you ever noticed that certain types of experiences provoke a profound flow of emotion, and you're not entirely sure why? And you are overwhelmed. And you weep or you cheer or you're so filled with wonder you're speechless. And you are carried away, transported just for an instant, to a different world. And then it passes, and you are back in your own world once again.

I spoke earlier of an intense longing in our souls, a hunger that nothing in this world ever seems to satisfy. I told you the thirst is never quenched because we have been made for another world. Once in a while, though, something happens that gives us a taste of that world. And even though those moments are fleeting, they are real, windows into a different realm.

Like Narnia's wardrobe, there is a magical doorway that allows us passage from the temporal to the transcendent—where we touch a bit of eternity. Different people have different doorways. I used to listen to Puccini arias, transfixed by their beauty. Italian is a language I do not speak, so my mind did not interfere with the intense emotion the music evoked. For others, an encounter with nature touches that deep place within, or a line of poetry, or a simple piece of prose, or a fragrance in the air briefly noted, that triggers the secret longing—something teased, but not satisfied.

I don't know what touches you that way, but I'm convinced we all experience it. Those moments are short-lived, and we quickly return to our standard state of longing. But those moments are real. We were made for something far better than what we experience in this life. And we know it. And we long for it. And once in a while we get a taste, a glimpse, of something eternal, just the faintest bit, before it quickly fades.

The next time you see something—a moment in a film, or an embrace, or a vista that transfixes you—or you hear something—a poem, or a melody, or a bit of a story—or you detect a faint fragrance that sends you, in the same moment, both back to a forgotten time and forward to a new, unknown one—and you find that deep down inside of you something moves and you are transported, and you want to weep, though you're not sure why—I want you to think, in that moment, that God is giving you a foretaste of Glory.

And one day we will lay hold of it in its fullness. The war will be over. The anguish will end—all brokenness mended, all evil vanquished, all beauty restored. We will be, once again, "naked and not ashamed."

For those who receive mercy, the home we have been seeking all of our lives will be ours. It is the Father's house, and there is a place for us in it.[17] And he will say, "Come. Enter. Enjoy. Be with Me."[18] And when he does we will realize (if there ever was, really, any question about it) that our hunger for home was always our hunger for him. And we shall have him.

And that will be the end of the Story, the true Story, the Story of Reality. But it will not be the end, of course. It will only be the beginning of a new one, one we have been waiting for all of our lives. I cannot tell you anything more about that since it is completely beyond me, except this: In that Story, we will experience life better than the best we ever thought possible since—above all other mercies—we shall be his, and he shall be ours. Forever.

Epilogue

I BEGAN THIS BOOK by making a promise, of sorts. First, I told you there are reasons for the way things are, that when we ask the question "Why?" about things that really matter—about the big questions of life—there are answers to those questions.

I said that understanding the big picture of Christianity, the Christian worldview—what I called the picture of reality—helps us to see how everything in the world that is significant fits together: how the world began, how it ends, and everything deeply important that happens in between. I went on to suggest, little by little, that no other picture of the world would do if you are going to find the answers you are looking for when you ask the questions that matter most.

I told you the true picture of reality is like a puzzle made up of many pieces. And, just like any other puzzle, you need to have all the right pieces put together in the proper way to see the picture clearly. If you are missing major pieces, or have pieces from other worldview "puzzles" mixed in, then you will not get an accurate picture of reality.

I also said that another way of looking at a worldview is thinking of it as a story. All worldviews follow a certain structure: creation, fall, redemption, restoration. All good stories follow a similar structure: beginning, conflict, conflict resolution, ending.

As we moved through our story, I tried to show you how the Christian Story takes all of the important pieces of the puzzle—things we discover by paying close attention to the world around us, true things we know deep down inside our hearts, and other things only the Author himself can tell us (and he does)—and puts them together in a tale we would never have guessed. It is not a story we would have thought up on our own. It is the Story the Storyteller himself has enabled us to discover from the clues he's left behind for everyone to see, and from the words he has spoken for those who will pay attention to them. It contains all the right parts of a complete worldview, and all the parts of a good story. Moreover, it helps us to see the role we play in the drama.

I also made a second promise. It's tied to two "clues" we are all able to pick up without any help from the Author. First, we all know that something is terribly wrong with the world. Things are not the way they are supposed to be. Second, we all know that something is terribly wrong with us. We are not the way we are supposed to be, either. There is evil in the world, and there is evil in each one of us.

This is where the second promise comes in. It has to do with the two biggest objections people have about Christianity—the problem of evil and the "narrowness" of the message. I said that once you understand the Story correctly, you'll see that the challenges of evil and suffering, and the singular solution the Story offers are not really the problems people think they are. The brokenness of the world and the unique role of Jesus are connected. They go together, hand-in-hand. Evil is not foreign to the Story, but is central to it. Indeed, the entire Story is about how human beings went bad, how our badness caused the world to go bad, and how both get fixed by God. It is the reason Jesus came to earth.

Sometimes when a story is a bit long (like ours is), it's helpful to go over it in brief to refresh our memories. It helps us see how the whole Story holds together with all the parts properly connected. It also helps us know if I have kept my promises.

The Story starts with God. He is the central character, the One the Story is all about, the rightful Sovereign, the ruler over everything he has made—the King over his Kingdom. The world he creates consist of things we can see, but also many things we cannot see. Both are real in God's world. He is a King, but he is also a Father, and we were made for friendship with him. The world he made was filled with goodness and purpose, and everything worked together just as God intended—no discord or unhappiness, no unmet needs, no disorder or distress or alienation.

Man, the second most valuable and important thing in all the world, is not a little god—he is a creature—but he is not junk, either. God made us beautiful in a way no other creature could be. Deep within our invisible selves, our souls, lies a special mark—the image of God, himself. Our God-likeness makes each one of us—regardless of age or size or ability or appearance—wonderful in a way that can never be taken from us. Because we alone bear the mark of God, we each have absolute value, deep worth, and ultimate purpose. This built-in value is the reason we are to be good toward others and the reason we have special privileges some have called "unalienable rights."

Though humans are beautiful, we are also broken—not physically, but morally. We feel guilty, because we are guilty. Man was not like this in the beginning. However, he used the good freedom God gave him to do something bad. He did not use his liberty to choose obedience—and thus grow in goodness—but to choose rebellion—and thus fall into death, darkness, and slavery. He went from freedom to bondage, enslaved to his fallen self and to the devil who tempted him. When Adam and Eve rebelled against the King of the universe, they not only broke themselves, they broke the whole world. That is the reason there is evil and suffering among us.

Worse than anything else, though, man's friendship with God was broken, too. Man's disobedience cut him off from God and, because of man's rebellion and betrayal of friendship, God was angry. He does not destroy man, though. Instead, as a humble act of kindness and grace, God himself steps down out of heaven into history in the person of Jesus to initiate a rescue operation.

The two indispensable things you need to know about Jesus have little to do with his teachings in general. Instead they have to do with who Jesus was and what he came to accomplish, also known as the person and the work of Christ.

Jesus was a true human being, just like you and me. But there was something more. He was the Word made flesh, the unique God-man, the

King of the universe who came down and got low for us. Jesus did not come to spread social justice, but to live the life we ought to have lived, then to trade his perfect life for our rotten ones. That trade happened on a wooden cross on a crop of rock outside the walls of ancient Jerusalem—a place the locals called Golgotha, the skull.

Jesus was crucified by Romans at the request of the Jews for claiming to be their king, the charge posted at the top of his cross. The greater anguish for Christ, though, is not the brutality he feels at the hands of men, but the punishment inflicted by the Father for a different list of crimes—our crimes, also "posted" on that cross—until the King's anger is spent, his justice is satisfied, and Jesus' task is finished. Jesus takes our guilt so that we might have his innocence; he takes our sin so that we might have his goodness. That is the trade, the gift offered by grace, to be received in simple trust to restore our friendship with God. When we trust him, we are born anew inside, "plugged in" once again to God, our only source of genuine life.

For now, God extends his hand of mercy, offering free forgiveness for sin and pardon to rebels. He will not delay dealing with evil forever, though. His patience will give way to action. In the end, all will be raised, the rebellious to perfect justice, the penitent to perfect mercy. The heavens and the earth will be remade, and evil will be no more.

So the Story ends with everyone living forever. Those who continue in rebellion forever banished to a place of misery, darkness, and utter loneliness and ruin. Those who cease their rebellion, who lay down their arms and surrender to their rightful King—who receive his pardon, who become members of his family—live with him in a new world enjoying the perfect life with him he intended for them at the first.

That is the Story about how the world began, how the world ends, and everything deeply important that happens in between: the beginning filled with goodness, the rebellion, the brokenness, the rescue, the trade, the mercy, the final justice, the end of evil, the ultimate restoration to perfect goodness, and—for those who trust the Rescuer—the unending friendship with a Father who, finally, satisfies the deepest longings of their hearts.

The Story has five elements: God, man, Jesus, cross, and resurrection. It's a story I can tell in a single sentence, though it's a bit long. Here it is:

God, the Creator of the universe, in order to rescue *man* from punishment for his rebellion, came to earth and took on humanity in *Jesus*, the Savior, to die on a *cross* and rise from the dead, so that in the final *resurrection* those who receive his mercy will enjoy a wonderful friendship with their sovereign Lord in the kind of perfect world their hearts have always yearned for.

If you are a Christian, this is your story. If you are not a Christian, this is also your story, because this isn't a religious fairytale. This is the Story of the way things really are.

But now you may be at a kind of crossroads. You have one of two choices. You can bend your knee to your Sovereign, beg for mercy because of Christ, be welcomed into his family as a son or daughter, and belong to him. Or you can reject the gift, stand alone at the judgment, and pay for your own crimes against God, such as they are.

I invite you to accept your pardon now, while you can, and turn and follow Jesus. Because this is not just a story. It's a true story. It's *the* true Story. It's the Story of Reality.

Notes

Chapter 1: Confusion

1. The idea that this story is the story all fairy tales are really about came from Clay Jones.
2. I am grateful to Chuck Colson for the insight that Christianity is a view of reality. His exact words were, "Christianity is not just a relationship with Jesus. It is a way of seeing all of life and reality" (from an interview on *Focus on the Family*, August 13, 2009).

Chapter 3: True Story

1. As G. K. Chesterton put it, "In one sense, of course, all intelligent ideas are narrow. . . . A Christian is only restricted in the same sense that an atheist is restricted. He cannot think Christianity false and continue to be a Christian; and the atheist cannot think atheism false and continue to be an atheist." *Orthodoxy* (Nashville: Sam Torode Book Arts, 2011), 19.
2. I am referring here to the famous ancient parable of the six blind men in India who encounter an elephant for the first time. It is often used to argue that different religions do not actually conflict. Rather, each represents part of the larger truth about God. I have written an article about this confusion titled "The Trouble with the Elephant." You can find it by searching for it by name at str.org.

Chapter 4: Two Obstacles

1. Jesus' comments about the "narrow way" can be found in Matt. 7:13–14, and His claim to be "the way, the truth and the life" can be found in Jn. 14:6. His disciples repeated the idea in many places, notable Acts 4:12 and Rom. 10:1–4, 9. Find a hundred such verses collected in the booklet *Jesus, the Only Way—100 Verses*, available at str.org.

Chapter 6: In the Beginning

1. The word "Genesis," the name of the chapter that starts the Story, means "beginning." It tells us about the beginning of everything that is most important to the storyline. It tells us about the beginning of the world, the beginning of man, the beginning of man's problem, and the beginning of the solution to his problem. Of course, there are lots of other interesting things that happened at the beginning that the Story never addresses, leaving many of our questions unanswered. That's because the Story doesn't intend to tell us everything, only the things important to its plot.

2. For the parts of the Story written to those suffering, look for the sections called Hebrews, 1 Peter, 1 and 2 Thessalonians, and Revelation, for example.

3. C. S. Lewis's point about God's ownership can be found in *Mere Christianity* (New York: Simon & Schuster, 1952), 59.

4. Some will recognize my paraphrase of Augustine's famous insight from his *Confessions*: "You have made us for yourself, and our hearts are restless until they can find rest in you."

5. Physical activity is happening in your brain at the same time you are thinking, of course, and is connected to your thoughts in complex ways, but those physical processes are not *the same thing* as your thoughts. They have completely different qualities.

6. The "He is there, and He is not silent" insight comes from Francis Schaeffer, who wrote a fine book by that title.

7. Note that this is the first issue addressed in the Westminster Shorter

Catechism. "What is the chief end of man? Man's chief end is to glorify God, and to enjoy him forever."

8. Jesus of Nazareth said, "Come to me, all who are weary and heavy laden, and I will give you rest. Take my yoke upon you and learn from me, for I am gentle and humble in heart, and you will find rest for your souls. For my yoke is easy and my burden is light" (Matt. 11:28–30 NASB).

Chapter 8: Matter-Ism

1. These words launch what is probably the most famous science documentary of all time, PBS's The Cosmos, hosted by the late astronomer Carl Sagan. Oddly, the defining concept of the series is not scientific at all. No empirical analysis can ever tell us all that ever was, or is, or will be, even in principle. No, Sagan's starting point is not a conclusion of science, but rather a presumption of philosophy meant to fix the boundaries of the world at the edge of the physical universe. It's what philosophers call a metaphysical doctrine, which is a way of describing what turns out to be a kind of religious dogma. That doesn't mean it's false (that would depend on other facts). It only means that the statement is not science. Indeed, I don't think the religious ring to the theme line is accidental, as it mimics a Christian doxology known as the "Gloria Patri."

2. Since the basic idea here is that reality consists of "nothing but" the physical, material world governed by "nothing but" natural law, C. S. Lewis called this the "nothing buttery" view.

3. The "mankind is the result of a purposeless and natural process" is a famous comment taken from the writings of George Gaylord Simpson found in The Meaning of Evolution rev. ed. (New Haven: Yale University Press, 1967), 344–45.

4. The Richard Dawkins comment can be found in River Out of Eden (New York: Basic Books, 1996), 133.

5. The "eat or be eaten" quip came from Jewish intellectual, Dennis Prager, who was pointing out the limitations of materialism.

Chapter 9: Mind-Ism

1. Francis Schaeffer, *He Is There and He Is Not Silent* (Wheaton, Ill.: Tyndale, 2001), 8.

2. Of course, not everyone who is concerned about the environment deifies nature in an everything-is-God kind of way.

3. Rhonda Byrne, *The Secret* (New York: Atria Books, 2006), 164.

4. I don't know about you, but it's hard for me to get excited about a religious system that teaches a cycle of reincarnation that even Jesus of Nazareth has not yet been able to escape from. I say this because it is not uncommon to hear of gurus—experts in this spiritual approach—who claim to be reincarnations of Jesus. Setting aside the problem that they can't all be Jesus' reincarnation living at the same time, there is something inherently discouraging about this claim. Though Jesus was arguably the most virtuous person who ever lived, he still has not been able to escape the painful, tedious cycle of reincarnation for 2,000 years. What hope is there for us commoners if even Jesus of Nazareth is still in the system working off his *karma* after two millennia?

5. Find a thorough description of both Hindu Mind-ism and New Age Mind-ism, along with their important differences in James Sire's *The Universe Next Door* (Downers Grove. Ill.: InterVarsity, 2004).

6. Byrne, *The Secret*, 183.

7. C. S. Lewis made the "thrills of religion" observation in *Mere Christianity* (New York: Macmillan, 1943), 21.

8. From Deepak Chopra and can be found, for example, on the web in "Coincidence or Higher Power? Three Experts Weigh In."

Chapter 10: Options

1. The idea that God is good, but not safe, comes (somewhat indirectly) from Mr. Beaver in C. S. Lewis's *The Lion, the Witch, and the Wardrobe*. Some might think it odd that God's goodness could also be a threat, but I think that concern will be resolved as the Story unfolds.

Chapter 11: Beautiful

1. The idea that man is completely different in a fundamental way from everything else in the created realm is what Francis Schaeffer called the "mannishness" of man.

2. "They exchanged the truth of God for a lie, and worshiped and served created things rather than the Creator—who is forever praised. Amen" (Rom. 1:25).

3. The Hebrew words *nephesh* and *ruach* (translated "soul" and "spirit" in the Old Testament), and the Greek *psyche* (translated "soul" in the New Testament) are all used of animals (Gen. 1:30, Eccl. 3:21, Rev. 8:9). We also know from common experience that pets have personalities (with thoughts, sensations, rudimentary acts of will, and so on) and are not simply biological machines like plants. There does not seem to be any reason, though, to believe that animal souls survive the deaths of their bodies the way human souls do. In this, humans seem to be unique.

4. Even though lately some have been confused on this difference between humans and animals, there is no reason for the rest of us to be confused.

5. The Jewish story—which the Christian Story is grounded in— contains this element too.

6. "You will fill me with joy in your presence, with eternal pleasures at your right hand" (Ps. 16:11).

Chapter 12: Broken

1. The "nobility and cruelty" way of stating man's dilemma comes from Francis Schaeffer in *He Is There and He Is Not Silent*, chapter 2, "The Moral Necessity," in *The Complete Works of Francis Schaeffer*, vol. 2 (Wheaton, Ill.: Crossway, 1982).

2. The "social contract" explanation for morality is actually a form of relativism critiqued more thoroughly in *Relativism: Feet Firmly Planted in Mid-Air* by Francis Beckwith and Gregory Koukl (Grand Rapids, Mich.: Baker, 1998).

3. This whole business of evolution being somehow responsible for beliefs of various sorts is an odd one to me. Pretty much all Darwinism has to work with is genes, and genes direct physical characteristics, not mental content. It's not clear that it makes any sense, then, to say genes dictate a person's beliefs about right and wrong. If that were true, you could no more choose your values than you could choose your eye color, but that's clearly not the way things work.

4. G. K. Chesterton, *Orthodoxy* (Nashville: Sam Torode Book Arts, 2011), 10.

5. Yes, there can be false guilt, of course, but only because there is real guilt that it imitates.

6. Jesus said, "Anyone who looks at a woman lustfully has already committed adultery with her in his heart" (Matt. 5:28), which is not the same as actual adultery, obviously, but is still a serious wrong.

7. "Jesus replied: 'Love the Lord your God with all your heart and with all your soul and with all your mind.' This is the first and greatest commandment. And the second is like it: 'Love your neighbor as yourself.' All the Law and the Prophets hang on these two commandments" (Matt. 22:37–40). One's "neighbor," Jesus pointed out elsewhere, includes one's mortal enemy, as the Samaritans were for the Jews. See Lk. 10:29–37.

Chapter 13: Lost

1. "He has also set eternity in the human heart" (Eccl. 3:11).

2. The "Terrible Lie" concept came from *The Jesus Storybook Bible* by Sally Lloyd-Jones (Grand Rapids, Mich.: Zondervan, 2009), 28. This is a first-rate Bible storybook for youngsters.

3. This idea of "the great separation of a man from himself" comes from Francis Schaeffer, *Genesis in Space and Time* in *The Complete Works of Francis Schaeffer*, vol. 2 (Wheaton, Ill.: Crossway, 1982), 70.

4. Find a clear expression of the significance of the unseen forces and the unseen realm in Eph. 6:10–12.

5. Job 5:7.

Chapter 14: Evil

1. Ancient philosopher Epicurus offered the classical form of this challenge: "Is [God] willing to prevent evil, but not able? Then He is impotent. Is He able, but not willing? Then He is malevolent. Is He both able and willing? Then whence evil?"

2. See my remarks on atheism and evil in chapter 4.

3. Of course God can make a bachelor who *gets* married—which in some cases seems like an impossible task—but then he would not be a married bachelor, just someone who *used* to be a bachelor and who now is married.

4. This is the very point made by a famous twentieth-century atheist in his argument against God. See J. L. Mackie, *The Miracle of Theism* (Oxford: Clarendon Press, 1982), 150.

5. When one of his young daughters told him she wanted to be happy, Larry Arnn, president of Hillsdale College, said, "You're too young to be happy. First you must learn to be good."

6. God created man with moral innocence—that is, there was no bad in him at all—but not with the kind of native goodness God himself has. God is good through and through, so to speak. Goodness is inseparably bound up with his nature. Man, however, needed to learn goodness by developing virtue over time through obedience.

7. I have proposed a *possible* way of resolving the conflict—a version of the "free will defense." Others have suggested different ideas. The point is this: Since there are *possible* solutions to the question of God's goodness and power and the existence of evil, then there is no *necessary* contradiction between them, and this is all that is needed to successfully parry this particular challenge.

8. Philosophers sometimes call the "was-it-worth-it?" concern— whether the total sum of evil and every instance of evil can be justified by some greater good—the "inductive problem of evil."

9. The elephant and the flea idea was suggested to me by Gregory Ganssle in his excellent—and wonderfully accessible—introduction to the philosophy of religion, *Thinking about God* (Downers Grove, Ill.: InterVarsity, 2004).

10. In the Story, Joseph's misfortunes, first at the hands of his brothers and then with Potiphar's wife, eventually put him in a position to rescue the fledgling nation of Israel from starvation. Late in life he saw his woes from a completely different perspective than at first: "You intended to harm me, but God intended it for good to accomplish what is now being done, the saving of many lives" (Gen. 50:20). C. S. Lewis also does a fine job of playing this point out in fictional form in his book *The Horse and His Boy*—a boy, beleaguered since birth, saves a kingdom precisely in virtue of the "evil" events he was forced to endure over time.

11. The point about God being good and wise may be controversial to some. I have only hinted at my reasons so far and have not really made the case. Briefly, God's wisdom can be inferred from the way he made the world. God's goodness can be inferred from the moral law he has written on our hearts. Without it, we would not be able to know that the world is morally broken to begin with.

12. The "our Story is not over yet" insight came from Devin Smith, my daughter's fine teacher at Beacon Hill Classical Academy.

Chapter 15: Wrath

1. This is the reason Jesus said, "You must be born again" (Jn. 3:7). Only a supernatural rebirth of our souls will allow God's life to flow back into us.

2. Regarding the grip this Prince of Darkness has on the world and his powerful deceptive influence, see 2 Cor. 4:3, 2 Tim. 2:26, 1 Jn. 5:19, and Rev. 12:9 and 13:14.

3. Ps. 14:3.

4. A majority of Americans believe in hell, apparently, yet almost none thinks he's going there.

5. "So the Lord God said to the serpent . . . 'I will put enmity between you and the woman, and between your offspring and hers; he will crush your head, and you will strike his heel'" (Gen. 3:14–15).

Chapter 16: History

1. The "folklore plagiarism" idea was first suggested in 1906 by Sir James Frazer in his book *The Golden Bough*.

2. For citations of primary-source information on pagan mystery-religion figures see Ronald Nash, *The Gospel and the Greeks—Did the New Testament Borrow from Pagan Thought?*, 2nd ed. (Phillipsburg, N.J.: P&R Publishing, 2003); Lee Strobel, *The Case for the Real Jesus* (Grand Rapids, Mich.: Zondervan, 2007); and Komoszewski, Sawyer, and Wallace, *Reinventing Jesus—How Contemporary Skeptics Miss the Real Jesus and Mislead Popular Culture* (Grand Rapids: Kregel, 2006).

3. Tryggve Mettinger, *The Riddle of Resurrection—"Dying and Rising Gods" in the Ancient Near East* (Stockholm: Almqvist & Wiksell International: 2001), 221.

4. *Futility* was the initial title of Morgan Robertson's book. It was later renamed *The Wreck of the Titan* (First Rate Publishers, 1898).

5. Lewis's actual statement, "You must show *that* a man is wrong before you start explaining *why* he is wrong," can be found, along with an extended explanation of his point, in *God in the Dock* (Grand Rapids, Mich.: Eerdmans, 1970), 272–3.

6. The historical material for Jesus' life includes more than what we find in the Gospels, though these provide the main body of information. It turns out there are at least seventeen primary source historical references pertaining to Jesus that lie outside of the Gospels. For details see, among others, Gary Habermas, *The Verdict of History* (Nashville: Thomas Nelson, 1988), 108. The significant material on Jesus found in these secular sources is just one more nail in the coffin of the recycled-redeemer theory.

7. Will Durant, *Caesar and Christ*, vol. 3 of *The Story of Civilization* (New York: Simon & Schuster, 1972), 557.

8. Luke had no firsthand acquaintance with Jesus, but rather researched his account from those who were eyewitnesses. See Lk. 1:1–4.

9. See 1 Jn. 1:1–3 and Acts 26:25–26.

Chapter 17: The God-Man

1. Jesus' moral and theological views were not, in general, original to him but were drawn from the wisdom of the ancient Hebrew prophets.

2. "So the Lord God said to the serpent . . . 'I will put enmity between you and the woman, and between your offspring and hers; he will crush your head, and you will strike his heel'" (Gen. 3:14–15).

3. Jesus was tempted in all ways, just as we are, but He never gave in to sin. Being sinful is not part of our "essential humanity," though it is characteristic of all humans, other than Jesus, since the fall.

4. See Jn. 8:58, Mk. 2:5–10, Jn. 5:23, Jn. 5:22, Jn. 6:35, and Jn. 11:25.

5. Jn. 11:25–26.

6. These "daring" sayings can be found in Jn. 8:24 NASB, Jn. 8:58, Jn. 12:45 NASB, and Jn. 3:18 NASB, respectively.

7. Peter's confession is in Matt. 16:16, and Jesus' claim at his trial can be found in Matt. 26:63–66.

8. Jn. 7:46.

9. Paraphrase of Mk. 4:35–41.

10. Jn. 1:1, 3 NASB.

11. Jn. 1:14 NASB.

12. Though the notion that God would become a man is not stated explicitly in the Hebrew Bible, there are hints of it in the writings of the Hebrew prophets. Note, for example, Is. 9:6 NASB: "For a Child will be born to us" (Jesus' humanity), "a Son will be given to us" (Jesus' deity). Or Micah 5:2 NASB: "But as for you, Bethlehem Ephrathah . . . from you One will go forth for Me to be ruler in Israel" (humanity). "His goings forth are from long ago, from the days of eternity" (deity).

13. To be most precise, God does not change into a man. Rather, he adds a human nature to his divine nature in the man Jesus.

14. That Jesus is one person with two natures, undiminished deity and true humanity, is called the "Chalcedonian formula" from the Council of Chalcedon in 451 AD. This unique merging of the Divine nature with a human nature is called the "hypostatic union."

15. The deliberations of the Great Councils that I mention resulted in refined statements about God's nature—like the Nicene Creed, the Chalcedonian Creed, and the Athanasian Creed.

16. C. S. Lewis, *Mere Christianity* (New York: Simon & Schuster, 1952), 136.

17. John Stott, *The Cross of Christ* (Downers Grove, Ill.: IVP, 1986), 158.

18. Phil. 2:5–8.

Chapter 18: The Rescue

1. The term *social justice* is misleading. The poor only need justice if they have been wronged in some way. Otherwise, the Story teaches charity and mercy toward those in need. The view that all poor people are victims is a recent invention. It is not what Jesus taught, and it is not part of the Story.

2. The single reference in John to the poor is found in Jn. 12:8: "You will always have the poor among you, but you will not always have Me."

3. Find the Sermon on the Mount in Matt. 5–7; the Bread of Life Discourse in Jn. 6; the Olivet Discourse in Matt. 24, Lk. 21, Mk. 13; and the Upper Room Discourse in Jn. 13–17.

4. Jesus makes a reference to the poor in Lk. 4:18–19 NASB: "The Spirit of the Lord is upon Me, because He anointed Me to preach the Gospel to the poor. He has sent Me to proclaim release to the captives, and recovery of sight to the blind, to set free those who are oppressed, to proclaim the favorable year of the Lord." Even here, though, it seems clear that, in light of the rest of the verse and everything that follows about Jesus' teaching on "the Gospel," He is making reference to spiritual benefits, not material benefits.

5. Lk. 18:9–14.

6. Hypocrisy (Matt. 6:2–3), a widow's generosity (Lk. 21:2–3), Zaccheus's repentance (Lk. 19:8), the rich young ruler's confusion (Matt. 19:21), a lesson about the afterlife (Lk. 16:20, 22).

7. Heb. 10:5–7.

8. Matt. 1:21, Lk. 2:11, Lk. 1:76–77, Jn. 1:29 NASB.

9. Jn. 3:17, Lk. 19:10, Lk. 5:32, Jn. 10:17–18 NASB, Matt. 20:28.

10. Jesus saves us from the Father, but His intention is not at odds with the Father since it was the Father who, out of love, sent Jesus to rescue the world in the first place.

11. Matt. 10:28 NASB; *"It is a terrifying thing to fall"*: Heb. 10:31 NASB.

12. The idea that the incarnation is a kind of invasion of enemy-occupied territory comes from C. S Lewis in *Mere Christianity*.

13. Heb. 10:5.

14. Jn. 21:25 NASB.

15. John Stott, *The Cross Of Christ* (Downers Grove, Ill.: IVP, 1986), 231.

Chapter 19: Footsteps

1. Born in Bethlehem (Micah 5:2) between 2–5 BC according to the reckoning of our current calendars, as best as we're able to determine from ancient documents.

2. The angel Gabriel (Lk. 1:26–38); the heavenly heralds at Jesus' birth (Lk. 2:8–14); the words of Simeon and Anna in the temple (Lk. 2:21–38); and the visit from the magi (Matt. 2:1–2).

3. Jesus' first miracle was at the wedding at Cana (Jn. 2:11). Jesus surprised his neighbors who had watched him grow up an ordinary boy (Lk. 4:22, Matt. 13:54–56).

4. Jesus "grew in wisdom and stature and in favor with God and men" (Lk. 2:51–52).

5. See Lk. 2:46–49.

6. Jn. 1:29.

7. For the Sermon on the Mount, see Matt. 5–7.

8. See Jn. 2:24–25.

9. See Jn. 5:18, 7:1, 19.

10. The Jewish leaders clearly understood that Jesus' claims to be the Son of God were, according to the way of speaking of the time, direct claims to divinity. See Jn. 5:18, 10:33.

11. The leaders attribute Jesus' power to Satan. See Matt. 12:22–29.

12. See Matt. 11:20–24.

13. Jesus' parables obscure his meaning from the unrepentant. See Matt. 13:10–17.

14. For The Bread of Life Discourse, see Jn. 6:1–71.

15. The crowds want to take Jesus by force and make Him king. See Jn. 6:15.

16. One of Jesus' disciples "is a devil." See Jn. 6:70.

17. Contrast the tax collector's humble admission of guilt with the spiritual pride of the religious person in Lk. 18:9–14.

18. See Matt. 23:27.

19. Find Peter's confession that Jesus is the Christ in Matt. 16:16.

20. The Transfiguration is in Matt. 17:1–8.

21. See Mk. 9:9–10.

22. See Jn. 11:47–53.

23. See Jn. 10:17–18.

Chapter 20: The Trade

1. Many think Jesus' hands were nailed through the palms, but archaeological evidence indicates this was not the practice. Spikes through the center of the hand would not hold the body's weight. The Scriptural references to his "hands" being pierced (for instance., Jn. 20:20) are accurate, though, since the wrists were considered part of the hand.

2. Jn. 19:19. "The written notice of the charge against him read: The king of the Jews" (Mk. 15:26).

3. http://bible.org/question/ what-does-greek-word-8216itetelestaii'-mean.

4. Col. 2:13–14.

5. Find the great judgment in Rev. 20:11–15.

6. "But I tell you that every careless word that people speak, they shall give an accounting for it in the day of judgment" (Matt. 12:36).

7. "There is nothing concealed that will not be revealed, or hidden that will not be known" (Matt. 10:26 NASB).

8. "Each person who is judged by his own behavior is found guilty." See Rev. 20:13–15.

9. "You are justified when you speak and blameless when you judge" (Ps. 51:4B).

10. "When the centurion, who was standing right in front of Him, saw the way He breathed his last, he said, 'Truly this was the Son of God'" (Mk. 15:39 NASB).

11. Jn. 19:30 NASB.

12. This is John Stott's translation given the perfect tense of the verb indicating an action completed in the past with results continuing into the present. John Stott, *The Cross of Christ* (Downers Grove, Ill.: InterVarsity Press, 2006), 84.

13. 2 Cor. 5:21.

14. 1 Pet. 3:18 NASB.

15. Eph. 1:7.

16. I picked up this wonderful anecdote somewhere in my distant past, but I do not know where, so I cannot properly credit the author, only thank him for it.

17. Is. 53:4–6.

18. Augustus Toplady (1740–78), "From Whence This Fear and Unbelief."

19. See Jn. 3:16.

20. See Eph. 2:8–9.

Chapter 21: Trust

1. The official term for the error of misrepresenting someone else's view, then attacking the distortion instead of the real thing, is "straw man fallacy."

2. Acts 2:22, Acts 1:3 NASB, Jn. 10:38, Jn. 20:30–31. Italics have been added for emphasis. This last verse follows immediately after Jesus' encounter with "doubting Thomas," making it certain that Jesus was not championing blind faith against Thomas's appeal for evidence. Thomas had plenty of reason to believe his friends' testimony, making his demand to actually touch Jesus' wounds before he would believe a bit extreme.

3. Ancient Christians used a three-part formula to describe the process:

knowledge, assent, and trust, what they called *notitia, assensus,* and *fiducia.*

4. The discussion on faith, reason, and evidence has been adapted from Gregory Koukl, *The Ambassador's Guide to Postmodernism* (Signal Hill, Calif.: Stand to Reason, 2009).

5. I think I first heard this way of putting it from David Horner. For those who think that reason and faith are opposed to each other, consider this. The opposite of faith is not reason, but unbelief. The opposite of reason is not faith, but irrationality. It certainly is possible to have a reasonable faith, and it is also possible to have an unreasonable unbelief. (I'm thankful to David Noebel of Summit Ministries for this observation.)

6. See 1 Cor. 15:14–19.

7. Jesus had more to say about truth than about faith. See Jn. 4:24, Jn. 8:32, Jn. 17:17, Jn. 18:37, Jn. 1:14, Jn. 14:6.

8. C. S. Lewis, *Mere Christianity* (New York, Scribner, 1952), 114.

9. See Rom. 5:1–2.

10. This is the meaning of the word *propitiation*—God's justice is satisfied because his wrath is spent. See 1 Jn. 2:1–2.

Chapter 22: Four Facts

1. Some scholars prefer an AD 30 date.

2. Evidence that the Gospels were written by close associates of Jesus can be found in Richard Bauckham, *Jesus and the Eyewitnesses* (Grand Rapids. Mich.: Eerdmans, 2006), and Michael Kruger, *Canon Revisited—Establishing the Origins and Authority of the New Testament Books* (Wheaton, Ill.: Crossway, 2012), among others.

3. These are not the only sources of historical information about Jesus, but they are the main ones.

4. You will find that warning near the beginning of chapter 13, "Lost," in the section starting, "The Story tells of a garden and a tree and a snake."

5. A host of works exist making the case for the historical reliability of the Gospels, such as Gary Habermas, *The Historical Jesus* (Joplin,

Mo.: College Press, 1996); William Lane Craig, *Reasonable Faith* (Wheaton, Ill.: Crossway, 2008); Craig Blomberg, *The Historical Reliability of the Gospels* (Downers Grove, Ill.: InterVarsity, 1987).

6. There is 75% consensus on the empty tomb and virtually 99% agreement on the other three facts. Find superb summaries of this approach in Habermas and Licona, *The Case for the Resurrection of Jesus* (Grand Rapids, Mich.: Kregel, 2004), 43–80, and William Lane Craig, *Reasonable Faith*, Third Edition (Wheaton, Ill.: Crossway, 2008), 348–400.

7. Habermas and Licona, 60.

8. See Gary Habermas, 158–67.

9. See Mk. 15:44–45.

10. See Jn. 19:38–40.

11. See Habermas & Licona, 70.

12. See Matt. 28:13.

13. William Lane Craig, 373.

14. William Lane Craig, 381.

15. Acts 2:32 NASB.

16. Rom. 1:4 NASB, Rom. 4:25 NASB, Rom. 8:1, 34 NASB.

Chapter 23: In Between

1. Deut. 29:29.

2. See 2 Pet. 3:9.

3. See Matt. 28:20.

4. Jn. 16:33 NASB.

5. This idea came from C. S. Lewis in "The Weight of Glory."

6. My thanks to Josh Runyon for this insightful way of putting it. I found it in Holly Ordway's excellent memoir of her spiritual journey, *Not God's Type* (Chicago: Moody, 2010).

Chapter 24: Perfect Justice

1. See chapter 20, "The Trade."

2. Any sin committed against man is first a sin against man's Maker. See Ps. 51:3–4.

3. The tormented ghost who visited Ebenezer Scrooge in the opening pages of Charles Dickens's *A Christmas Carol*.

4. See Jn. 5:22, Acts 10:42.

5. See Jn. 3:17.

6. Rev. 20:11–13, 15.

7. 2 Thess. 1:9 NASB.

8. See James 1:17.

9. See Matt. 8:12.

10. See Lk. 16:23–24.

11. Mk. 9:48 NASB.

12. Dominique Bouhours 1628–1702, *Pensées Chretiennes*, cited in Hugh Hewitt, *The Embarrassed Believer* (Nashville: Word Publishing, 1998), 142–3.

13. Richard Wurmbrand, *Tortured for Christ* (London: Hodder & Stoughton, 1967), 34.

14. C. S. Lewis, *Mere Christianity* (New York: Simon & Schuster, 1943), 24.

Chapter 25: Perfect Mercy

1. See Rom. 8:23.

2. See Rev. 21:10 to 22:1–2.

3. C. S. Lewis, *The Weight of Glory, and Other Addresses* (New York: HarperCollins, 1949), 29.

4. See 1 Pet. 1:3–9.

5. See Heb. 10:17 NASB, Is. 1:18 NASB , 1 Cor. 6:11.

6. 1 Jn. 3:2.

7. See Rom. 8:29.

8. See Rev. 21:4.

9. See Rev. 21:23–25 and Rev. 21:4.

10. See 2 Cor. 4:16–18.

11. See Rev. 21:1.

12. The apostle Paul tells us that sin is falling short of the Glory of God (Rom. 3:23). If in the resurrection we will never sin again, then we will always manifest the Glory of God himself.

13. See 1 Cor. 15:50.
14. See Lk. 24:39.
15. See 1 Cor. 15:40–49, 1 Jn. 3:2.
16. See 1 Thess. 4:13–18.
17. See Jn. 14:2–3.
18. See Ps. 23:6.

Acknowledgments

A HOST OF PEOPLE DESERVE credit for any fruitfulness this work affords to its readers. Many will note the influence of three authors—remarkably capable Christian thinkers—who've had a profound impact on my thinking as a Christian and, therefore, on this work and on my life. They are C. S. Lewis, Francis Schaeffer, and J. P. Moreland. I am deeply beholden to each.

It's hard to overestimate the debt I owe to four people at Stand to Reason for their superb editing skills. In addition to being wonderful cheerleaders, each made a unique and singular contribution to the final form of this book: Nancy Ulrich for her considerable capability in all aspects of editing, especially wordsmithing; Amy Hall for her help with word choice, structure, and logical flow; Melinda Penner for her all-around wisdom and insight; and Ocean Wilson for her eagle eye at copy editing.

Michael Horton, Gary Habermas, Fred Sanders, Douglas Groothuis, and Michael Licona gave me valuable academic feedback on critical portions of the book. I am fortunate to have counsel from the very best in their respective fields.

Ryan Pazdur and the very capable team at Zondervan were always helpful, professional, insightful, cooperative, encouraging, and (thankfully) patient. They were wonderful to work with, always open to suggestions, and always going the extra mile to make this book the best it could be.

Mark Sweeney, my matchless literary agent, made everything about writing and publishing a book so much easier. He was like a coach to me through the whole process—urging me forward, smoothing the way, fixing problems, giving counsel, cheering me on—gentle all the while.

Finally, but of first order, "my girls"—my wife, Steese Ann, and my daughters, Annabeth Noelle and Eva Rae—who I thank from my heart for their patience with the process and for "loaning me" for hours without number to my eventual readers.

Tactics Study Guide with DVD

Gregory Koukl

In a world increasingly indifferent to Christian truth, followers of Christ need to be equipped to communicate with those who do not speak their language or accept their source of authority.

In the *Tactics Study Guide with DVD*, apologist and radio host Gregory Koukl demonstrates how to get in the driver's seat in discussions about faith, keeping any conversation moving with thoughtful, artful tact. Readers will learn how to maneuver comfortably and graciously through the minefields, stop challengers in their tracks, turn the tables, and—most importantly—get people thinking about Jesus with conversations that look more like diplomacy than D-Day.

Drawing on extensive experience defending Christianity in the public square, Koukl demonstrates how to:

- Initiate conversations effortlessly
- Present the truth clearly, cleverly, and persuasively
- Graciously and effectively expose faulty thinking
- Skillfully manage the details of dialogue
- Maintain an engaging, disarming style even under attack

The *Tactics Study Guide with DVD* provides a game plan for communicating the compelling truth about Christianity with confidence and grace.

Tactics

Gregory Koukl

In a world increasingly indifferent to Christian truth, followers of Christ need to be equipped to communicate with those who do not speak their language or accept their source of authority. Gregory Koukl demonstrates how to get in the driver's seat, keeping any conversation moving with thoughtful, artful diplomacy. You'll learn how to maneuver comfortably and graciously through the minefields, stop challengers in their tracks, turn the tables, and—most importantly—get people thinking about Jesus. Soon, your conversations will look more like diplomacy than D-Day.

Drawing on extensive experience defending Christianity in the public square, Koukl shows you how to:

- Initiate conversations effortlessly
- Present the truth clearly, cleverly, and persuasively
- Graciously and effectively expose faulty thinking
- Skillfully manage the details of dialogue
- Maintain an engaging, disarming style even under attack

Tactics provides the game plan for communicating the compelling truth about Christianity with confidence and grace.

Available in stores and online!